DEATH
ON THE
VICTORIAN
BEAT

THE SHOCKING STORY OF POLICE DEATHS

This is Constable 195, Hugh Chesworth, who served in the Salford Police between 1877 and 1901. He is my great-grandfather and this book is dedicated to his memory. It is also for his great-great-great-grandsons, William and Matthew Baggoley.

DEATH
ON THE
VICTORIAN
BEAT

THE SHOCKING STORY OF POLICE DEATHS

MARTIN BAGGOLEY

PEN & SWORD HISTORY

First published in Great Britain in 2018 by
PEN AND SWORD HISTORY
an imprint of
Pen and Sword Books Ltd
47 Church Street
Barnsley
South Yorkshire S70 2AS

ISBN 978 1 52670 592 1

Printed and bound in Great Britain by TJ International Ltd, Padstow, Cornwall

Typeset in Times New Roman 12/14 by
Aura Technology and Software Services, India

Pen & Sword Books Ltd incorporates the imprints of Pen & Sword
Archaeology, Atlas, Aviation, Battleground, Discovery,
Family History, History, Maritime, Military, Naval, Politics, Railways,
Select, Social History, Transport, True Crime, Claymore Press,
Frontline Books, Leo Cooper, Praetorian Press, Remember When,
Seaforth Publishing and Wharncliffe.

For a complete list of Pen and Sword titles please contact
Pen and Sword Books Limited
47 Church Street, Barnsley, South Yorkshire, S70 2AS, England
E-mail: enquiries@pen-and-sword.co.uk
Website: www.pen-and-sword.co.uk

Contents

Acknowledgements

I owe thanks to Laura Hirst of Pen & Sword and my editor Carol Trow for their encouragement and support and to the staff of the Archives and Local History department at Bury Library for the help they provided.

Introduction

When Queen Victoria came to the throne in the summer of 1837, the foundations of the modern police force that we know today had been established. However, it had been a lengthy process and was not yet complete. In eighteenth century London, Sir Henry Fielding had created the Bow Street Runners and later, the Marine Police Force came into being. Nevertheless, much of the country still relied on a motley collection of unwilling elected or inept constables and inefficient night-watchmen.

As the nineteenth century approached, it was becoming widely recognised that a professional police force was necessary. Industrialisation was having a dramatic impact as agricultural workers and their families moved into the growing towns and cities, in which crime was very much on the increase. In 1800, the Glasgow Police Act led to the establishment of the Glasgow City Police, which was paid for by a local tax, as the inhabitants had become concerned at the rapid growth in crimes against property and the person. Similar fears resulted in the formation of the Irish Constabulary with the passing of the Peace Preservation Act of 1814. Discussions had been ongoing for a number of years regarding a force for London, which resulted in the formation of the Metropolitan Police in 1829. Significant developments followed throughout the remaining years of the century, but one principle never changed, which was that officers should remain largely unarmed, a fact I was constantly reminded of when writing the book.

Watch Committees, which became responsible for maintaining good order by appointing paid constables, were introduced with the passing of the Municipal Corporation Act of 1835. The immediate effect this approach to policing had is evident in the chapter dealing with the death of Inspector Ross in Liverpool in 1838, when he was ordered to assist in putting a stop to an unauthorised prize fight in a public place, which the old watch had always refused to do. The aggressive response of the crowd which had gathered to watch the fight, also serves as an example of the hostility with which the police were viewed by many in those early years.

Another important landmark was the introduction of detectives by the Metropolitan Police in 1842. This was hugely controversial as the idea of police officers in civilian clothes led to the early detectives being regarded as nothing more than spies, acting on behalf of an oppressive state. In 1856, the County and Borough Police Act required the Justices of the Peace in any county in which a constabulary did not exist, to ensure that one was introduced, thus creating a truly national force covering England and Wales. This development was welcomed by many as the initial antagonism shown towards the early police had by now abated.

What became clear when researching the book is that as the role of the police officer changed, the dangers he faced increased not just in the urban districts, but also in the countryside. For instance, throughout much of the century, there were many serious confrontations with poachers, which is discussed in the chapter concerning the double murder of Inspector Drewitt and Constable Shorter at Hungerford in 1876. Urban police officers faced danger during what were becoming increasingly violent industrial disputes and in 1862, Constable Jump met his death in a strike by brick makers at Ashton-under-Lyne. Furthermore, those seeking an independent Ireland, by violence if necessary, brought their struggle to the mainland and in 1867, Sergeant Brett fell victim to them in Manchester.

The police have always been required to intervene in domestic arguments and public order matters, in which violence is an ever-present possibility. This danger is highlighted in the case of Constable Menhinick, who met his death when called to a drunken argument in Holcombe in 1876. What also became clear was that very rarely, fellow officers could pose a threat and such a tragedy is remembered in Ballinadrimna in 1892.

I have included cases from across the country together with the killings of members of the Special Constabulary and others employed on the capital's docks and by a northern railway company. The courage and commitment to duty demonstrated by these unarmed men, who lost their lives, becomes evident on every page and as I looked into their deaths, I did not come across one significant call to arm the police from colleagues or the bereaved families. Of course, all the police victims in the book are male as it would be several years before women were able to serve in the office of constable.

Martin Baggoley

1

Acting Inspector William Horner Ross
Liverpool Town Police
1838

The Liverpool Town Police came into existence on Monday 29 February 1836 under the terms of the Municipal Corporations Act 1835 and the first meeting of the new Watch Committee was held a few days later. A report had been commissioned into the state of crime in the town, which was to be presented at that meeting, to assist the committee members to decide on the force's priorities.

The report focused very much on the problems associated with the district's 300 brothels and several hundred disreputable public houses, beer shops and low drinking dens known as 'taps', many of which remained open outside of the permitted licensing hours and well into the early hours of every morning. They were said to be the haunts of prostitutes and the receivers of stolen property, without whom the district's estimated one thousand professional thieves would be unable to dispose of their ill-gotten gains. It was anticipated that the new professional and hopefully well-regulated force, which had replaced the previous inefficient and badly managed group of constables, would at last restore some order to the town.

Members of the Watch Committee were also aware that for many years complaints had been made regularly by the area's more reputable citizens about the unsavoury characters who had gathered in certain areas, often in broad daylight and the failure of the constables to take effective action against them.

One such area was Toxteth Park and in June 1835, the *Liverpool Mercury* contained a report of large groups of youths gathering

Toxteth Park in the early nineteenth century. (The author)

there, especially on Sunday mornings. They used foul language, gambled at games such as marbles and pitch and toss and fights were not uncommon. Furthermore, local residents were harassed and threatened, especially young women, who were subjected to lewd comments. The article ends on a rather sarcastic note, with the suggestion that the constables at least, were keeping to the Sabbath by not patrolling the area and leaving it free for the worst of the town's inhabitants.

When out on patrol, the new police officers were therefore encouraged to adopt a proactive role by moving on these individuals and arresting those who refused to do so. This served to exacerbate the sense of resentment felt among the lower classes, who believed the very existence of their haunts and traditional practices and pastimes were under threat. The first major incident stemming from this fear occurred on a night towards the end of June 1836. Constable William Brown was on Dale Street and came across a crowd of about two hundred people, one of whom he could see, was brandishing a knife. The constable rapped the ground with the feruled end of his staff to give notice that a police officer was approaching. With the staff, he tapped the man holding the knife on the shoulder and demanded

2

that he place it on the ground. However, the man, Michael Dillon, a coachman, lunged at the constable and inflicted a serious wound to his left arm. He then attempted to flee but was detained by the injured officer and a colleague, who had arrived at the scene.

Despite the very serious nature of the injury, the constable survived and Dillon was charged with wilfully and maliciously stabbing him, which was a capital offence. At his trial, the accused man insisted he had no memory of the incident as he had been hit on the head earlier that evening and recalled arming himself with the knife in order to be able to defend himself. He was found guilty, but the jury added a strong recommendation for mercy in view of what they believed was his excited state of mind and the judge agreed with them. Dillon was formally sentenced to hang but was subsequently transported for life. It would be another two years before the first Liverpool police officer would die whilst on duty.

It was eleven on the morning of 8 June 1838, that a hearse drawn by four horses, left the grounds of the Infirmary, carrying a coffin containing the body of Acting Inspector William Horner Ross, to begin its journey to the Mount Cemetery. The inspector had lost his life some days earlier, having been beaten with such savagery that he did not survive. The hearse was accompanied by his weeping family and friends, together with almost four hundred police officers, including thirty inspectors and the Head Constable. Many of the town's residents lined the streets along the route, silent and their heads bowed to show their respect. The procession reached the cemetery at twelve forty-five and the interment took place

It is clear from a poem, which had appeared in the *Liverpool Mercury* two days earlier, that the dead officer was respected and admired by his colleagues;

LINES ON THE DEATH OF ACTING
INSPECTOR ROSS
BY A POLICE CONSTABLE
'Tis true he has fall'n - our champion in danger –
Brutality's victim!-he sleeps with the dead;
But he fell in his duty, and fear was a stranger
Unknown to the bosom whose spirit is fled.
We have borne his remains to the bed of his fathers,

And light lies the sod on his motionless breast,
Where the tempest storm comes not, and tumult
ne'er gathers
To break his repose in the valley of rest.
Though deep the regret that thy comrades may cherish,
For one so belov'd, so respected by all,
Thou hast won a 'promotion' that never can perish,
As laurels that fade, in the land of the pall.
And shall we not, Ross, ere misfortune may sever
The friends who admire thee – how soon may it be!
Raise a stone o'er thy ashes, though humble so ever,
And dew it with tears as we ponder on thee.

On 14 August 1838, seven young men were led into the dock at the Liverpool Assizes. James Macklin (23), it was claimed 'did cast and throw against the ground the inspector and with a large stick, beat him about the head, sides and back' and that Patrick Cunning (18), Edward Connolly (21), James Durning (18) and Martin Murphy (26), 'did while the inspector was on the ground, feloniously beat, strike and kick him, giving him thereby divers mortal strokes, wounds and contusions whereof he languished until 6th of June, when he died'. George McCarty (19) and Patrick Moorland (20) were accused of aiding and abetting the others. All pleaded not guilty.

Toxteth Park had been the site of many illegal bare knuckle prize fights in the past, which were attended by large numbers of spectators and on these occasions, the old local watch had not intervened. The new police however, were determined to put a stop to them and when information was received that one was about to start there at six o'clock on the evening of 28 May 1838, the inspector and two constables, John McQuan and William Cowan were very quickly at the scene.

A large crowd had already assembled to watch the contest, which was being promoted by Cumming, Connolly, McCarty, Durning and Murphy. It had not yet started and Inspector Ross ordered those present to disperse, telling them that if they did not do so, reinforcements would be sent for. However, he was ignored and the spectators, encouraged by the promoters, began to form a ring as

Illegal prize fights were popular and well attended events. (The author)

the two fighters stripped to the waist. The inspector sent Constable Cowan to seek assistance and he returned a little later with Inspector George Wharton and several constables.

By this time, three rounds had been completed, but realising there was now a much larger contingent of police, the two fighters attempted to run away. However, Wharton gave chase and detained one of them, which provoked an angry response from many in the crowd. The promoters, who were later arrested at the scene, played a significant role in the events that followed. Wharton was able to give details of the attack made upon himself and the eyewitness accounts of three constables, Robert Richie, Thomas Threlfall and John McQuan proved to be important in revealing what happened to Ross.

Wharton described being confronted by Connolly, who struck him with a large stick, knocking him over. His attacker released the detained fighter who made good his escape. As he lay on the ground, the inspector was kicked repeatedly by Connolly until he became unconscious. It took him several minutes to recover and when he did, he learnt that Ross had been taken to the Infirmary, given the seriousness of his injuries.

Constable Richie told the court of an angry mob throwing stones at him and his colleagues and shouting 'Kill the police' repeatedly. He saw Macklin grab hold of Ross from behind, before kicking his feet from under him and forcing him to the ground. Richie's account of what followed was supported by constables Threlfall and McQuan. Connolly struck the inspector at least twice to the head with a stick and the others accused of his murder continued to kick him as he lay helpless and unable to defend himself. All agreed that McCarty and Moorland took no active part in the assault, but they did urge the others on. There were also two civilian witnesses who were able to corroborate the officers' accounts. Margaret Barwood lived close to the scene and saw the attack on the deceased, as did Robert Bowerbank, a carter working in his employer's stables. Both of these witnesses implicated all five of the defendants charged with participating in the actual assault.

An attempt to rescue the inspector was made by his colleagues but they were driven back by the crowd. It was not until more officers arrived some minutes later that he was finally pulled free and it was then that the severity of his injuries became apparent. He was taken immediately to the Infirmary, where he was treated by surgeon, John Nottingham. He testified that there was extensive bruising to the whole of his patient's body and five serious wounds to his head, all of which were consistent with the inspector having been the victim of a serious assault. After a few days he suffered inflammation of the brain, which was the cause of death.

All of the accused called character witnesses who spoke well of them. In their defence it was argued that in the confusion in those few minutes, the evidence of the crown witnesses could not be relied upon. In his summing up, the judge explained the difference between manslaughter and murder and also raised the possible problems which might arise from relying on evidence of identification only. The jury retired for forty-five minutes before returning with manslaughter verdicts in respect of all the defendants except for Moorland who was found not guilty of any offence and was freed immediately.

The judge told those remaining in the dock that although convicted of the less serious offence, their crime was committed 'under circumstances of great disorder and cruelty and their victim, who was acting in the discharge of his duty, was defenceless'. He continued by telling them that if they had been convicted of murder, he would have selected just one of them, Macklin, for execution to serve as an example to others. He sentenced all of them to be transported for life.

2

Special Constable William Tilsley
Spernall
1842

William Crowley's farm was on the estate of Sir Robert Throckmorton, at Spernall, four miles north of Alcester in Warwickshire. Sadly, his relationship with his youngest son, 31-year-old James, had been poor for several years. James believed that he had been treated unfairly by his father and this sense of injustice had only intensified with the passing of time. It was an issue that had gripped the small rural community in which they lived and there were many who supported the son's claims, especially after James published a sixteen-page pamphlet in which he outlined his grievances.

In the pamphlet, he told of how in 1832, his father offered him a share of the business, but subsequently failed to fulfil his promise. Rather than offering compensation of some description, he began to treat him in an even more appalling manner, apparently now intent on injuring his reputation, interests and happiness, whilst promoting those of his brother Joseph and his family. As the dispute intensified, family friends offered to attempt to bring the differences of father and son to an amicable end, but James stated that his father refused the offer.

Of his father, James wrote:

> 'His mind is replete with envy, hatred and malice towards me; nor can he think well of anything I do, whether in look, word, thought or action – everything is condemned before any advance is made. It is actually incredible, the distinction that is made between my

brother, my nieces and nephews and myself. They are all treated with the utmost kindness and indulgence, in fact they are idolised. But the treatment I receive from my father differs as much from that as black does from white.'

Their relationship continued to deteriorate to such an extent that James was heard to threaten his father's life and he would then commit suicide. In late March 1842, James was ejected from the family home, but his father agreed to pay him £1 weekly and to provide him with a horse and its feed. James moved into a cottage three hundred yards away. However, his father told other family members and friends that he feared what his son might do to him. It was against this backdrop that a decision was made to provide William with some protection. 20-year-old William Tilsley, who stood six feet tall, was a married man with two children and he lived in nearby Sambourne. He was considered to be mature and sensible and worked on William's farm. He was sworn in as a special constable with one specific purpose, that of protecting his employer from his son.

On 22 December 1842, James approached his father in an extremely threatening manner and William was so concerned that he asked his protector to visit his son to warn him not to behave in such a way again. This was done, but it was agreed that the special constable should have breakfast and dinner with the Crowley family on Christmas Day, lest James should decide to visit the house to spoil the occasion, as he knew most of his family would be there. Those fears proved to be justified.

Early on Christmas Morning, James called at the farmhouse and threatened once again to shoot his father. Tilsley told him, 'You had better leave him alone, you had better be quiet.' James did leave, but glaring at his father said, 'I will see you another day about this old gentleman.' As he was walking back to his cottage, his mother followed him and begged him to stay away, but he simply repeated the threats against his father.

As noon approached, Mrs Crowley was looking through the window and saw James riding towards the house, carrying a double barrelled shotgun. She cried out to her husband, 'James is coming, for goodness sake, go upstairs,' and grabbing him by the arm, forced him to do as she said.

On reaching the house, James used his gun to smash a window and utter more threats. The sound of breaking glass alerted Tilsley and Joseph Street, who was with him at the rear of the building. The two men made for the front, where they were joined by 14-year-old John Nicholls, who was returning home after attending church. The three of them confronted James, who on seeing them screamed 'What, you are coming are you?' and immediately raised the gun, firing one barrel into the special constable's left eye. His face was destroyed and his head shattered into pieces. Looking down at his victim's corpse, James said, 'Now you'll do.' He then turned towards Joseph and John and pointing the gun at them shouted, 'I have shot one and I will shoot you if you do not take care.' They ran to the stable as James mounted his horse and rode off.

Mr Morris, a surgeon, arrived at the farm later that afternoon and performed a post-mortem, the result of which was predictable. The shot had exited at the back of the head and a large amount of blood, bone and brain had emerged from the massive wound.

The inquest opened a few days later in the Marlborough's Head Inn at Studley, after the members of the coroner's jury had viewed the body. The dead man had been a well-known and respected young man in the district, which given the nature of his injuries, made it an upsetting experience for the jury. They later heard from those present at the shooting and the final witness was William Crowley. He gave details of the family history, which led the coroner to ask if James had shown any signs of insanity in the past, to which his father replied that in his opinion there had been none. The jury found that the deceased had been wilfully murdered by James, who was still at large. The coroner announced he would be writing to the Home Secretary, recommending that a reward be offered for his capture. At the close of the inquest, Tilsley's body was taken to his father's house at Sambourne to await burial a few days later at Coughton.

A reward of £40 was offered for information leading to the fugitive's arrest and his description and that of his horse was circulated across the country. It was learnt that later on Christmas Day, he passed through Stratford-on-Avon and then rode to Shipston-on-Stour, where he left his horse. He was next seen on a coach to London, after which he disappeared. In the months that followed there were rumours that he was in various places, which included Redditch, Liverpool and America. However, as the months passed and no arrest was made, it was assumed by many that he had committed suicide as he had threatened to do in the past.

However, he had not done so as he had indeed travelled to America but had returned to England in March 1844 and settled in Chester. In late December of that year he was arrested at his lodgings in the Castle and Falcon on Watergate Street. He had been betrayed to the authorities by a young woman he had promised to marry, but who he had later abandoned. He appeared before the magistrates in Stratford-on-Avon and was committed to stand trial at the next Warwickshire Assizes.

The trial, which lasted two and a half hours, took place on 31 March, by which time James's father had died. The accused did not deny killing the special constable, describing it as an unfortunate accident and a not guilty plea was entered. The crown witnesses were not challenged by his barrister, who in opening the defence, insisted his client was insane. This infuriated the prisoner, who had not been told this would be done and it took some time to calm him down.

A number of character witnesses were called, who described him as an essentially good man who was devastated by what he perceived as the wrongs of his father. The jury also heard from his brother William, who spoke of a history of insanity within the family. He told of another brother, John, experiencing episodes of odd behaviour, which on one occasion had culminated in him stabbing himself in the stomach. Three of his sisters had also exhibited signs of insanity; Sarah had been confined in a number of lunatic asylums; Mary was said to have made several attempts to drown herself and was once saved by the accused; and Ann was described as being unbalanced.

When he addressed the members of the jury, the judge stated that when a plea of insanity was entered they must be satisfied that at the time of the crime, the accused could not differentiate between right and wrong. The jury retired for ninety minutes before returning with a guilty verdict. He was sentenced to death and the execution was scheduled to take place on 18 April at the Warwick County Gaol, but he still had a great deal of support from those who believed he had been treated unfairly by his family and a petition

Sir James Graham, the Home Secretary who refused to save the murderer. (The author)

seeking a reprieve was sent to Sir James Graham, the Home Secretary. As he awaited the decision, two of his brothers attempted to visit him in the condemned cell but he refused to see them and shortly afterwards he was advised that the petition had failed.

He woke early on the day of the hanging and ate a breakfast of eggs, toast and a glass of ale. He attended the prison chapel, after which he was pinioned and led out onto the gallows, around which a large crowd had gathered. Moments later he shouted, 'I am ready, I am prepared,' and the hangman withdrew the bolt. He died instantly and the body was left to hang for the usual hour.

There was a widely held belief that if a woman had her wens and other skin blemishes rubbed by the hand of an executed criminal, they would disappear. Several women paid the hangman to take advantage of this opportunity, which was a means of supplementing his fee.

Afterwards, when his papers were being removed from the condemned cell, the following note was discovered, which gave his version of events surrounding the murder;

'I resolved to return again to my father's house and claim my natural right of inheritance, the privilege of walking quietly and peaceably into it at my pleasure and the gun which unfortunately and accidentally produced the death of Tilsley, I took with me charged, capped and cocked, as it had been for several days previously, for the sole purpose of intimidating all parties from treating me with brutality or offering me any interruption, but when I arrived at the front door and found it secured against my entrance, perceiving my father and mother in the front kitchen, for the purpose of intimidating them, I thrust the muzzle of the gun through four or five panes of the window and instantly turned round and proceeded in the direction of the back door. But I had scarcely turned the corner, when I perceived four or five persons within a few paces of me running towards me. At the same instant, without speaking a word, I raised the gun, intending to have shot over their heads, but in my hurry and confusion, before I could get it to my shoulder, it accidentally exploded.'

If, as James had wished, this had formed his defence rather than the insanity plea, it seems unlikely that the jury would have been minded to reach a different verdict.

The hangman strokes a young woman with the hand of an executed criminal to rid her of skin blemishes. (The Newgate Calendar)

3

Detective Sergeant Charles Thain
City of London Police
1857

Born in Bavaria, Christian Sattler turned to crime as a youth and afterwards led a nomadic lifestyle. Following service in the French army in Algeria, he travelled to England, where he continued with his criminal ways. His preferred modus operandi was to book into a hotel and wait for an opportunity to steal from other guests.

In the late autumn of 1857 and now 37 years of age, he was coming to the end of a three months prison sentence in Wisbech Gaol in Cambridgeshire, for the theft of a large quantity of baby clothes. On the eve of his release he had a conversation with Benjamin Eason, the chief warder, who later recalled urging the obviously intelligent prisoner to find lawful employment and settle down. Sattler had replied by saying that no Englishman would hire him and continued by suggesting that rather than ask for poor relief, he would return to crime, adding if anyone attempted to stop him, he would 'Shoot him like a dog'.

He was released on 28 October and booked into the Golden Lion Hotel in St. Ives, Huntingdonshire, using the name Henry Smith. On 2 November, London stockbroker Arthur Ballantine, who was in the district to collect rents, arrived at the hotel, intending to stay for one night. His bag contained a few items of clothing, two razors and a gold breast pin, together with £234 in Bank of England notes. The stockbroker left the bag unattended briefly in his room and in those few minutes it was stolen.

Suspicion immediately fell on Henry Smith, who had booked out of the hotel soon after the theft. However, it was quickly realised he was in fact Sattler, who had been seen in the town earlier that day by local police officer, Superintendent Alexander Brown, who knew and recognised him. The superintendent was unaware he was staying at the Golden Lion but when the theft was reported, he told of the sighting and the search for Sattler began. The police were able to trace his movements as they had the serial numbers of the notes, which Sattler used to pay bills and to purchase a number of items over the next few days.

On the morning of the third, Sattler had visited the premises of Cambridge pawnbroker Robert Cole and pledged a mackintosh, subsequently shown to be Mr Ballantine's, for five shillings. He returned to the shop thirty minutes later, having possibly waited to see if the pawnbroker's suspicions had been raised and the police called. Satisfied it was safe to return, he bought a watch for six guineas and offered a £20 note in payment. Unbeknown to Sattler, Mr Cole sent his assistant with the note to his bank to check the number and was advised it was acceptable as details of the theft had not yet reached the town's banks. Mr Cole had seen his customer's wallet stuffed with banknotes and was told that the man's father had sent him the money from Glasgow. That night, Sattler booked into the Spread Eagle in Gracechurch Street in London and left the next morning. A chambermaid later found a shirt in the room, which was identified as having belonged to Mr Ballantine. Before leaving the district, Sattler visited the shop of chemist Daniel Church and purchased a number of items. He gave the name Christian Koch, but the notes used to settle his bill at the Spread Eagle and to pay the chemist, were part of the proceeds of the theft at St Ives.

The task of arresting Sattler was put in the hands of 45-year-old Detective Sergeant Charles Thain of the City of London Police, who with the assistance of his fellow detective, William Jarvis, learnt the suspect had left England for Hamburg. It was now mid-November and Thain travelled there alone, in possession of a warrant and on his arrival the fugitive was detained with the assistance of the local police.

There was no formal extradition agreement with the port's authorities, but at ten o'clock on the night of Friday 20 November, the handcuffed Sattler was escorted on board the *Caledonia,* an English vessel which traded between London and Hamburg, by Thain and several local police officers in plain clothes. This was witnessed by Stephen Robertson, a rescued shipwrecked mariner, who with government assistance was returning to his London home. He saw the Hamburg officers leave shortly afterwards and at ten thirty, as he was passing the cabin allocated to Thain and his prisoner, he heard Sattler complaining loudly, that the handcuffs were too tight on his wrists and were causing him a great deal of discomfort. Robertson was unable to sleep that night and from his berth at five o'clock in the morning, he again heard Sattler complaining that he was in pain. He also heard Thain reply that if he continued to behave himself he would consider removing the handcuffs.

Another passenger, James Whitelegg, saw the police officer with his prisoner out on deck the following day and noticed how considerate Thain was towards Sattler, although he was still wearing the handcuffs. Stephen Frost, captain of the *Caledonia,* visited the pair that day and on entering their cabin, he too was struck at the kindness shown to the prisoner by Thain, who was adjusting the handcuffs in an attempt to make them more comfortable. The captain, concerned for the well-being of his passengers and crew, insisted that the prisoner should remain handcuffed during the voyage.

Little was seen of them until four o'clock on the Sunday afternoon, when a gunshot was heard coming from inside their cabin. Stephen Robertson was first to arrive there and as the door was locked, he kicked it in to find the room full of smoke. Sattler was sitting quietly on a chest, a pistol at his side and Thain was on a bed, clutching at his chest and said, 'The prisoner has shot me.' Robertson turned to Sattler and asked why he had done so to which he replied, 'The officer broke faith with me and has not kept his word as a gentleman.'

There were a number of American sailors among the crew, several of whom were soon gathered in the cabin. They took hold of Sattler, who was handled very roughly and some of them who wanted to lynch him or throw him overboard, had to be restrained from carrying out their threat. A length of chain was found with which Sattler was secured to a ring bolt on deck, where he remained for the rest of the voyage, while the wounded detective was given medical assistance. Robertson approached Sattler and spoke with him for some time. The prisoner told him he had purchased the weapon in Hamburg

16

and Thain had taken possession of it when he arrested him and had locked it in his baggage. The detective had left the cabin for a few minutes and Sattler had taken the opportunity of breaking the case open, retrieving the pistol and loading it. When Thain returned to the cabin, he shot him.

After the *Caledonia* arrived in London, Thain was taken to Guy's Hospital and placed under the care of surgeon, Alexander McDougal, who realised the chances of the officer surviving were low. It was therefore arranged for a deposition to be taken from him on 28 November, by Mr Combe, a magistrate at the Southwark Police Court. Sattler was at the bedside as Thain gave the following account of the shooting:

'I am a City of London detective police officer. On the afternoon of 19th November instant, I had the prisoner in custody at Hamburg and this day last week we sailed on the Caledonia steamer from Hamburg to London. We were in a cabin, which I held the key of. Last Sunday, in the forenoon, the prisoner and I were in the cabin together. He complained of being ill and asked me to take the handcuffs off. I said I was not allowed to do it. He and I were in the charge of the captain, who would not allow me to do it. He said I had broken faith with him and I said that faith was not placed in my hands at sea, but when we arrived in England I would take them off if he behaved himself.

'We turned into our berths and at about twenty to four, I got up and left the cabin to go to the water closet, having locked the cabin and left him there. I returned in about a quarter of an hour and found he was sitting on a folding carpet stool, directly opposite the centre of the berth. I said "Mr Sattler, aint you going to have any tea today?" He said "No, I don't think I will". I had a Mackintosh cape in my hand and while I was in the act of placing it away, he stood up and all at once fired at me. I felt wounded in the right nipple and cried out "Murder". I laid hold of my bag, which was on my bed and laid hold of the prisoner and dragged him and told the men to secure him, as I was shot.'

That night, Sattler wrote a letter to his victim expressing regret for his actions and asking for forgiveness. However, he received no reply, as Thain died on 4 December and a post mortem was performed the following day. Three pistol balls were removed from his corpse and the singeing to his clothes confirmed that he had been shot at very close range and that the wound to his right breast had proved fatal.

Charged with the wilful murder of the detective, Sattler's trial opened at the Old Bailey on 4 January 1858. He entered a not guilty plea on the grounds that given the absence of an extradition treaty with Hamburg, he was not in legal custody and as the arrest was unlawful, he had the right to resist in any way necessary; at the very worst, he was guilty of manslaughter. The crown argued that it was open to any British subject to arrest a felon guilty of a crime committed in this country and furthermore, it was implicit in his stated motive for killing Thain, which was not to escape but because the officer had broken faith with him, that he was on the *Caledonia* voluntarily.

In his summing up, the trial judge agreed with the crown but acknowledged the jury might have some reservations and left it open to them to return a verdict other than wilful murder. The jury found him guilty of murder and he was sentenced to death. However, he was reprieved for three weeks as the defence took the matter to the Court of Queen's Bench.

The appeal failed as the higher court decided that although the accused was a foreigner, he committed an offence against English law and his conviction was correct. It was noted that he was on board an English vessel, which was part of the dominion of England and he owed obedience under these circumstances, to the laws of this country. However, he failed to do so as he killed a British subject on a British ship and it did not matter whether he was being held lawfully or unlawfully. Therefore, the conviction was correct and the death sentence could be carried out.

The hanging had been due to take place on 25 January but was postponed until February 8. Many believed this was done by the Home Secretary, because on the 25th, the queen's daughter, Princess Victoria was to marry Prince Freidrich Wilhelm of Prussia. It was

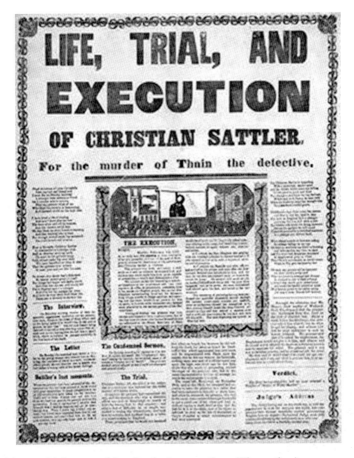

A broadsheet which was sold at Sattler's execution. (The author)

thought that the government feared the day would be spoiled by the ribald behaviour associated with public executions by the thousands of spectators who attended Newgate to watch them and this led to the decision to defer the punishment. This view is reflected in a letter sent to the *London Daily News*, which also suggests novel grounds for a reprieve for the condemned prisoner;

> 'It is painful to think this man, having been respited merely in order that the nation's joy on the late royal marriage might suffer no diminution (for it is idle to attribute the respite to any other motive) is now that

the rejoicings are over, to be executed. Monday next, the second hebdomadal return of the wedding day of our Princess Royal is appointed to take away the life of this man.

'Mercy is one of the divine attributes; it is also a queenly one. On every Good Friday, there is a custom for the sovereign of Spain to spare the life of at least one criminal under sentence of death. In the royal chapel of the palace are placed, close to the Cross on this occasion, the files of the proceedings against criminals condemned to die. The sovereign, in the act of adoration, takes into his hands one of these files, which signifies the granting of a pardon to the culprit whose trial it contains.

'There is a pleasing anecdote related to the young Queen Isabella II, that being but a girl when she for the first time took a part in this ceremony and on being informed of its significance, she took up all the files placed before her, by which act of grace a free pardon was extended to all the delinquents.

'Now sir, a free pardon is not desired, but surely one degree of mitigation in the sentence might be expected. It is not too late. There are circumstances which warrant a measure of mercy; nor can it be doubted that the occasion of the lately celebrated nuptials of England's Princess Royal affords a fitting occasion for its exercise in the present case. I am Sir, HOPE.'

The Home Secretary remained unmoved and there was no reprieve. Less than an hour before his execution, Sattler was handed a letter which had just arrived from his aged father in Bavaria, from whom he had long been estranged. In it he expressed regret that he was unable to travel to London to see his son, but said his thoughts were with him at this sad time and he sent his love. Shortly afterwards, William Calcraft, the hangman, led Sattler out onto the scaffold outside the gates of Newgate Gaol. He was calm and bowed twice to the waiting crowd. He bade farewell to the officials and at his request, the hood was not pulled down over his face. The drop opened and he appeared to die instantly.

Sattler was hanged outside the gates of Newgate Gaol. (The author)

Sattler was fortunate, for Calcraft's controversial 'short-drop' method, which involved the use of a shortened piece of rope, often led to the condemned prisoner suffering a lengthy and agonising death by strangulation rather than quickly due to a broken neck.

Thain had been a police officer for fifteen years and was much admired and respected by his colleagues who collected sufficient funds to have a monument erected over his grave in Highgate Cemetery in early 1859.

4

Constable William Jump
Lancashire Constabulary
1862

In the early 1860s, brick makers throughout the North West of England were involved in a protracted and increasingly bitter dispute with their employers over the hiring of non-union men. Large stocks of bricks were destroyed regularly, horses at work in the brick yards were maimed and a night-watchman was shot and seriously wounded. However, the violence reached its peak at Ashton-under-Lyne in Lancashire, at two o'clock in the morning of 28 June 1862, as Sergeant George Harrop and Constable William Jump walked across a field known locally as Small Shaw's Fold.

They saw a group of eight men enter the field and walk towards them in single file. Striking brick makers were known to be active in the district and the police officers became suspicious as the men appeared to be intent on hiding their faces and some could be seen attempting to conceal what the officers realised were large sticks, under their topcoats. Six of the men were allowed to pass, but the last two were stopped and challenged. The sergeant asked them what they were doing at large at that time of the morning and why were they carrying such sticks, which he suggested they could use as weapons. At first, the two men ignored the officers and attempted to push past but were prevented from doing so. There was a brief struggle, but the officers were able to hold on to them until one of the men shouted to his companions, 'Now men, now men, now.'

One of the others produced a pistol with which he shot the sergeant in the face, badly injuring his eye. There was a second shot which missed, but which was so close to hitting him that it scorched his face. Another of the men was by now fighting with Jump and warned him,

'If you don't allow me to pass, I'll blow your brains out.' This was followed by two more shots and the constable called out, 'Catch him,' as he fell to the ground. The men fled the scene and the wounded constable, who was bleeding badly, was carried to a nearby cottage, where he died a short time later. He was 29 years old and left a widow and five children.

An inquest was held at the town's Dog & Partridge Inn at which surgeon Samuel Lees told of being called to treat the constable but arriving too late to save him. He performed a post-mortem and confirmed death was due to two bullet wounds to the chest, which caused severe internal injuries. The deceased was well known in the area and at the conclusion of the hearing the coroner's jury donated their fees to a subscription fund in his name. When later opened to the public, a large amount of money was raised for his family.

It was learnt that shortly before the shooting a group of men had broken into the nearby brickyard of Joseph Clifford and destroyed eighteen thousand soft bricks by trampling on them. The path on which the shooting took place led from the brickyard and suspicion fell on members of the Ashton-under-Lyne branch of the Union Club of Brick Makers, which met regularly at the town's Globe Inn. This theory was given credence with the discovery of a significant piece of evidence in the field in which the shooting took place. This was a receipt bearing the name of Michael Burke, issued by local beer house keeper Joseph Knott, which had been used as wadding. He confirmed Burke was a regular customer and also a brick maker. The police enquiry was now focussed on the Globe Inn, which was visited and the union's records seized. This led to eight suspects coming to light and these were Michael Burke, John Ward, Frederick Hipwell, Thomas Barlow, Robert Ryan, John Henshaw, Samuel Gregory and John Toole. Nevertheless, there were no immediate arrests as all the men had left the district and the last three named individuals would never be found as they were believed to have fled to Ireland.

A watch was kept on a number of addresses of known sympathisers, one of which was at 133, Butler Street, Manchester, the home of John Clay Johnson, who made brick makers' shovels and was known as 'Shovel Jack'. Police noticed the curtains of the house remained closed for several days and Mrs Johnson was seen to leave the house and purchase large amounts of beer a number of times. The police decided to force their way in and discovered Burke and Ward hiding in a bedroom and took them back to Ashton-under-Lyne.

Johnson claimed not to have been aware they were in his house, insisting they must have entered without his knowledge. This account was supported by the two fugitives but unsurprisingly they were not believed and 'Shovel Jack' was charged with being an accessory after the fact. Hipwell and Barlow were also found and the former was charged with the policeman's murder together with Burke and Ward. However, Barlow took advantage of an offer of a pardon by agreeing to testify on behalf of the crown. Ryan was also arrested but it was felt that there was insufficient evidence against him and he was released without being charged. This decision was subsequently reversed and a warrant issued for his arrest, but by then he had left the country.

The trial of the three alleged murderers and Johnson, who faced the less serious charge, opened on Monday 25 August at the South Lancashire Summer Assizes in Liverpool. The crown began by advising the jury that the murder was a crime of common purpose, meaning that Ward, Burke and Hipwell were equally guilty, irrespective of who actually fired the fatal shots. Burke, it was claimed, could be placed at the scene due to the discovery of the receipt upon which his name was written. Evidence was also provided which put Ward there as his cap was found close to where the shooting took place and plaster casts made of boot prints leading away from the spot, were identical to a pair of his boots.

However, it was Barlow's testimony which proved crucial. He told the court of the eight brick makers meeting and arming themselves with pistols and bludgeons, which they all declared they were prepared to use if necessary. The witness had not seen the shots fired but said that he heard Ward and Burke both admit to the shooting when he was held with them in a cell at the Ashton lock-up following their arrests. Ward told him, 'I shot first,' but Burke had insisted, 'No I shot first.'

Furthermore, Hipwell distanced himself from the other two accused men and denied carrying a weapon. Also, he described seeing Burke hand the paper on which his name appeared, to Ward to be used as wadding. Part way through the trial, the crown conceded it did not have the same overwhelming evidence against Hipwell that they possessed against the other two. The jury convicted Burke and

Kirkdale Gaol. (The author)

Ward of murder but Hipwell was found not guilty and released. The two men were sentenced to death and Johnson was given eighteen months in prison with hard labour for his role after the murder. To widespread surprise, Burke was later reprieved and transported for life. On the eve of his execution, 36-year-old Ward met with his wife for the last time and expressed his delight that Burke had been spared the rope.

Ward was hanged outside the gates of Liverpool's Kirkdale Gaol on Saturday 13 September and standing at his side on the gallows was William Taylor, who had been convicted of murdering Manchester estate agent Evan Meller and who was also suspected of murdering his own three children. A crowd estimated to be between 70-100,000 spectators came to watch the event. Many had travelled in special trains from Ashton-under-Lyne and from across the region, while others walked to the gaol, including 400 who were allowed to sleep overnight in the grounds of the workhouse at Warrington as they made their way to Kirkdale.

The condemned men appeared calm as they walked out of the gaol and bowed towards the crowd, into which Ward threw his cap to great cheering and applause. Taylor was accompanied by Thomas Wright a well-known Manchester prison reformer and philanthropist, who offered to befriend and support those condemned to death for crimes committed in that city, often until their final moments. Ward stood for a few moments in prayer with Taylor, Mr Wright and the chaplain of the gaol before being dispatched without a struggle. The executioner was William Calcraft, an unpopular and controversial figure and as often happened, he was hissed by the crowd throughout the procedure. His response was to leap down into the pit, position himself between the two suspended bodies and as he held them steady, he pulled faces at the crowd.

There was a sad postscript to the executions, which came to light three days later at an inquest held before Liverpool coroner, Mr C.E. Driffield on the body of William Edwards, aged two months. William's mother had attended the executions and afterwards celebrated by drinking a large amount of alcohol with friends at a number of public houses. That night she shared her bed with William and hopelessly drunk, she rolled over on top of him. He was found dead the next morning, having suffocated underneath her. The outraged

William Calcraft, the hangman.
(The author)

coroner's jury was determined to return a verdict of manslaughter, intending that the dead boy's mother should stand trial. It was only with great difficulty that the jury members were persuaded to accept Mr Driffield's advice that it would be difficult to prove such an offence had been committed at any future trial. Thus, the official but controversial verdict was that William's mother had overlain him accidentally when drunk.

The often disorderly behaviour of the crowds and incidents such as the death of young William contributed to the steadily increasing support for the abolition of public executions. The idea that there was a deterrent value to them was losing credibility and the events surrounding the hangings of Ward and Taylor prompted an anonymous correspondent to express his or her feelings in the following letter to the editor of the *Manchester Chronicle*:

'If it is requisite to put a man to death, there are many compendious ways of doing it without hanging in public. Chloroform or prussic acid may revolt the public mind but that would be less offensive to decency than to hang a man up like a dog before a hundred thousand spectators. Such scenes as the one enacted on Saturday are horribly grotesque. Philanthropy marches first in the person of Mr Wright, too good a man to figure on the scaffold. Religion brings up the procession in the person of the surpliced chaplain with his 'Man that is born of women etc'. While midway walks Justice impersonated in Mr Calcraft, a fellow with whom neither religion nor philanthropy would shake hands – a wretch abhorred, detested, hooted down though he merely acts as a sheriff's substitute. The sacred trio perform their parts, the philanthropist shakes hands, the chaplain stops the liturgy and the culprits are turned off. Calcraft steadies their writhings with a professional touch, gives a parting grin at the crowd et exeunt omnes. Behind the scenes, matters are still more repulsive. The murderer in the course of a fortnight is talked into a matured saint; he is brought into such a happy frame of mind that the crime of which he has been found guilty and the death he is about to suffer, figure as the mercifully arranged antecedents to eternal happiness and the sacramental cup precedes pinioning as a passport to Heaven. Such are murder and hanging considered as branches of the fine arts. With such parentage we may firmly cling to the consolatory conviction that the arts themselves will never become extinct and that each succeeding generation of artists will vie with their predecessors in zeal, genius and proficiency.'

At the conclusion of the trial, the judge had commended Sergeant Harrop for his bravery and ordered that he be given a reward of

£10 from public funds. Also, the Chief Constable of the Lancashire force promoted him to the rank of inspector on his return to duty following a period of absence due to his injuries. Furthermore, on the evening of Friday 3 October, in the council chamber of the town hall, a presentation was made to him on behalf of the town's grateful residents, who had contributed to a collection at which he received an illuminated address, a gold watch and chain and a purse of gold.

In December 1867, Robert Ryan surrendered to the Ashton-under-Lyne police, having spent the previous five years in America, where he had fled on learning he was a wanted man. He explained that he was tired of life as a fugitive in a foreign land and wished to return to his home and family. He denied participating in the murder and was willing to face a jury. Unusually for a man charged with the murder of a police officer, he was granted bail until Tuesday 31 May 1868 when he appeared at the South Lancashire Assizes. He was found not guilty of the constable's murder but was sentenced to nine months imprisonment with hard labour for destroying bricks in Joseph Clifford's brickyard.

5

Constable Ebenezer Tye
East Suffolk Constabulary
1862

Constable Ebenezer Tye of the East Suffolk Constabulary was a 22-year-old single man who had served in the force for sixteen months. When he reported for duty on the night of 24 November 1862 at Halesworth Police Station, he and Sergeant Daniel Taylor discussed the recent spate of petty thefts, usually committed between five and seven o'clock in the morning, which had been reported in the town. A local man, 63-year-old John Ducker, a hay cutter and a known thief, was suspected of being responsible.

The constable was instructed to keep a watch out for Ducker in the town and to make occasional visits to his cottage and report any suspicious activity. Throughout the night, the sergeant met Tye at regular intervals, the last occasion being at four o'clock, but there was nothing to report as he had not seen Ducker. Tye later failed to return to the station at the end of his shift and on learning he had not been home, Sergeant Taylor, fearing for the officer's safety, ordered that an immediate search of the town should be made and Ducker questioned.

The sergeant's fears were well founded, as the missing officer's body was discovered at nine o'clock that night in two feet of water in a stream at the rear of Ducker's cottage in Clarke's Yard. Tye was lying face up with his right arm by his side and his left raised as though he had been attempting to push away an individual who was holding him under the water. Nearby were his hat, handcuffs and staff, which suggested he was attempting to arrest someone when he met his death. He was clearly the victim of foul play and his body was taken to the nearby Angel Hotel.

It was believed Tye must have approached his killer, who ran off and as the constable gave chase, he had taken out his staff and handcuffs. Catching hold of the suspect in the middle of the stream, there had been a violent struggle, during which Tye had been knocked down and held under the water until he died.

Ducker was more than forty years older than the deceased but he was a powerfully built man and the police had no doubt whatsoever that he was capable of committing the crime and that he was the murderer. He was arrested on suspicion of murder together with his friend and neighbour Stephen Warne, whose wife Emily was also detained. It was not believed that the couple had been involved in the murder itself, but they were thought to have helped Ducker after the crime.

That the suspect had been involved in a violent fight in the immediate past was confirmed by Frederick Harrison, a surgeon, who examined him after his arrival at the police station and found serious facial injuries. His eyelids were swollen and a dark livid colour; there were a number of deep scratches on his nose; his left cheek was cut and there was a large head wound. When asked to explain them, Ducker said the injury to his head was caused by the comb he had used that

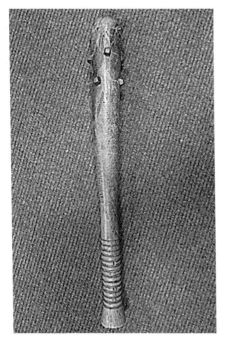

This cudgel was found among Ducker's possessions and he is believed to have used it when committing the crime. (The Suffolk Police Museum)

morning. The others were allegedly received on the previous Friday whilst he was cutting wood and splinters had flown into his face. Mr Harrison replied that he was talking nonsense, as a comb of any description would not have resulted in such a serious head wound, nor would chippings have caused the extensive cuts to his face. He added that anyway, all of the injuries were less than twelve hours old.

Mr Harrison also performed a post-mortem on the dead officer and an external examination revealed a bruised face and swollen neck but these would not have caused the constable's death. He had also suffered a serious blow to the head, which although not fatal, would have rendered him insensible. Following an examination of the stomach contents and lungs, the doctor concluded that whilst temporarily incapable of properly defending himself, he was gripped by the neck and held under the water until he drowned.

The stream in which the constable died was essentially an open sewer and the water was filthy, meaning Tye's clothes smelled badly. The police were satisfied they could show that Ducker too had been in the stream that same morning, having discovered incriminating wet and foul-smelling items of clothing in his cottage. His boots were wet and covered with mud similar to that in the stream; a pair of his dirty stockings was hidden under a bed; his mud-covered coat was under some straw; and a pair of trousers in a similar condition was retrieved from under a cushion.

Ducker denied the clothes had been hidden deliberately and under questioning insisted that on the Monday night, Benjamin Warne, father of Stephen, asked him for any old clothes he did not need, which he could let him have and it was the items in question he had given him. Ducker continued by saying he believed at the time that his neighbour wanted them permanently. Nevertheless, the following afternoon on arriving home, he found they had been returned and claimed Benjamin must have gained entry through the unlocked door to the property. He claimed that they must have been handed to Stephen, who was presumably wearing them when he committed the murder. Stephen denied any involvement in the crime and insisted Ducker was lying about the clothes, which neither he nor his father had been given or had taken.

Stephen and Emily Warne provided significant information, which helped the police greatly. They told of Ducker calling on them at eight thirty on the Tuesday morning with a dry but dirty shirt and asking Emily if she would wash it for him. One hour later the couple saw him burning another shirt in his yard. The police believed he was burning the shirt he wore when committing the crime and he needed the other shirt to be cleaned so he had that to wear in its place, as the search of his house had revealed he had very few clothes. The couple's evidence would prove to be important and it was now acknowledged they had nothing to do with the crime, which led to the charges against them being dropped and their release from custody.

Other neighbours gave information regarding what they had seen and heard between six and seven on the Tuesday morning. Hannah Tooke, a widow, reported seeing Ducker in the yard and a few minutes later she heard him arguing with Tye. She recognised both of their voices as she had often spoken with the friendly Tye and Ducker's speech was distinctive as he had lost his front teeth.

Elizabeth Sawyer was also a widow, who despite not looking out onto the Yard, had heard Ducker's footsteps which she knew well. These were followed by the sound of a scuffle, which ended with a man's groans, which were also heard by painter, Charles Todd. All of these neighbours had seen the suspect early on the Tuesday morning and later in the day, by which time he had changed his clothes and the police believed this was because those he wore in the morning would have been filthy and shown, on closer inspection, that he had been involved in a struggle in the stream.

Further damaging information was given by Benjamin and Stephen Warne. Stephen had been with Ducker on the previous Sunday night and the accused man had said there was some wood on a nearby farm, some of which he intended stealing over the next two or three days. He added ominously, 'I won't be stopped by one police. If there is only one he would go life for life.' Stephen took this to mean he was prepared to kill a policeman rather than be arrested. On the Tuesday morning at eight o'clock, Benjamin saw Ducker and noticing his swollen face, asked if he had been in a fight. Ducker replied, 'Yes I have. I had a scurry with the policeman.' No wood was found when Ducker's property was searched, but a truss of hay was discovered hidden away. It was believed Tye must have seen him carrying this and asked him to explain how it came into his possession, which led to the fight and its tragic outcome.

As his neighbours gave their statements at the inquest, which was held at the Angel Hotel, and also at Ducker's appearance before the town's magistrates, he interrupted them repeatedly. He accused them of lying and persisted in his attempt to blame Stephen Warne for the killing. Nevertheless, he was committed at both hearings to appear at the Spring Assizes in Bury St Edmunds to stand trial for wilful murder. At the conclusion of the inquest the coroner had released the constable's body and a few days later he was buried in Halesworth Cemetery. Many of his colleagues attended as did several hundred sympathetic townsfolk.

The trial took place over one day on 26 March 1863, by which time Ducker had received legal advice and it was now acknowledged that Ducker was responsible for Tye's death, but he pleaded not guilty to his murder. Following the presentation of the crown's evidence, which was similar to that given at the inquest and before the magistrates, his barrister began by simply dismissing his attempts to implicate members of the Warne family as something that was natural for a man in his situation to have done.

This was followed by an effort to dismiss the evidence of most of his neighbours, for it was argued they had contributed nothing of significance, as they had only heard what they believed to have been an argument between two men they had not seen. The Warnes had claimed to have damaging evidence against the accused, but they had given this at a time when they were believed to have been involved in the murder and they had concocted their account in an attempt to save themselves.

Criticism of the police followed as it was said they refused to consider other possible explanations of what occurred and were intent on making Ducker pay for killing their colleague. It was accepted that Tye had stopped Ducker, who was carrying the truss of hay and despite there being no evidence it was stolen, Tye had demanded that he give an explanation as to how it came into his possession. Any subsequent attempt to arrest him was illegal, especially if, as was evident from Ducker's facial injuries, excessive force was used. In such circumstances, Ducker was entitled to defend himself and had simply knocked the constable down into the stream, not intending any permanent harm. He did not hold him down, but walked away, unaware Tye was in any difficulty and in danger of drowning.

The trial judge did not dismiss this possibility in his summing up and told the jury a manslaughter verdict could be considered. Alternatively, if it was thought this was a case of justifiable homicide, a not guilty verdict was possible.

The jury retired at six thirty and after an absence of forty-five minutes returned to the courtroom and announced their verdict of guilty to wilful murder. The judge put on the black cap and told the now convicted man:

> 'John Ducker, you stand convicted after a careful trial of the crime of murder. The conclusion which the jury have been compelled to come to by the weight of the evidence is a conclusion that I, the judge, feel myself bound to concur in. The guilt of murder is brought home to you with this conviction, that the evidence seems to me to show that you resolved on a course of criminality and with deliberate

Several colleagues of Constable Tye gather at his grave to pay their respects. (The Suffolk Police Museum)

malice planned the murder of an officer of justice who was endeavouring to prevent you in that criminal course. I can hold out no hope to you in this world and I pray that you use the time that remains in making preparations for that future life which awaits you. The law commands me to pronounce the sentence of death'.

A petition seeking a reprieve was submitted to the Home Secretary and three members of the jury wrote a letter stating that despite believing murder was the correct verdict, they hoped mercy could be shown to the condemned man. However, these pleas were unsuccessful and two days before he was to be hanged, Ducker met with his two daughters and their husbands and his son in an emotional final meeting in the condemned cell.

It was during his last morning that Ducker admitted committing the crime alone and absolved the Warnes of any responsibility. The hanging was carried out by William Calcraft outside the gates of Ipswich Gaol, on 14 April 1863.

6

Sergeant Charles Brett
Lancashire Constabulary
1867

It was the night of 4 November 1867, three days after those convicted of involvement in the murder of Sergeant Charles Brett of the Manchester Police during the rescue of two leading Fenians some weeks earlier, had been sentenced to death. The crime took place on Hyde Road and it was feared those who had testified on behalf of the crown, many of whom lived close to the scene, might face reprisals. It had been decided therefore, that a number of police officers should patrol the area for the foreseeable future, to ensure no such attacks took place.

One of those witnesses thought to be at risk, was John Griffiths, whose barber's shop was on Hyde Road and who since testifying at the trial, had received anonymous threatening letters. Therefore, when Constable Daniel Connell noticed a young woman he did not recognise, peering into the shop window, he decided to investigate. He approached her and commented on the window display, to which she responded by asking if he was an Irishman. The officer told her he was not and he immediately heard a sound he recognised to be that of the hammer of a gun being cocked. He looked down and saw the woman was holding a pistol, which she was pointing at him but which had not fired.

As he attempted to take the weapon from her it broke into two pieces, the stock remaining in the woman's grasp, as the barrel came away in the constable's hand. She was detained with the help of some colleagues, who were nearby and taken to the local police station, where she was later identified as 19-year-old Adelaide Noble Macdonald.

The weapon was examined by Manchester gunsmith Thomas Newton, who confirmed it was loaded with powder, a wad and a bullet. If the pistol had been charged correctly, there was sufficient powder in it to have shot the constable, who would have undoubtedly suffered serious and possibly fatal injuries. It would appear that he owed his life to his would-be assassin's inexperience of firearms. A search of her lodgings revealed literature indicating her support for the Fenians, but the circumstances surrounding her behaviour led police to believe she had acted alone and was not part of an organised plot of any description.

It emerged that she had recently attempted to visit William Allen, one of the condemned Fenians being held in Salford's New Bailey Gaol but had been refused entry. She never revealed the nature of their relationship, but it was believed she did not know him very well, if at all, but had become infatuated with him after hearing of his actions on behalf of Irish independence and had decided to murder

Sergeant Charles Brett.
(The author)

John Griffiths for the major part he had played in identifying Allen as having been involved in the killing of Sergeant Brett. Her handwriting was compared to that of one of the threatening letters and was found to be similar. Part of the letter, which refers to two of the condemned men, read:

'Mr Griffiths, I can assure you, you will not stand in your door, for you will be shot like a dog and all your other confederates. You saw Allen fire did you? I can tell you, you will not live to see so many more revolvers. I will have your life. You will put your shutters up and have to keep them up. Your grave is dug ready. I bet you will identify no more Maguires. I will send you where your expenses will be paid and you will get the reward you are looking for and that is hell. We will put your light out – Yours 'A McMANNIS. P.S. – With confidence, so help me God. Don't alarm yourself to think what I say is not true, for everything I mean I will do, by the help of the brotherhood, who will arrive this week. The attack on the van will be nothing to that made on you, you elf of hell, damn you. Send all such of you and you will get your reward in style – a cap full of bullets through your skull, all the lot of you.'

In his testimony at the trial, Mr Griffiths told the court that he had not seen the defendant, Thomas Maguire at the scene of the rescue, so the author of this letter was probably referring to the 'Molly Maguires'. This was a secret society, active for much of the nineteenth century in the struggle for Irish independence.

Following her arrest, she told police she had decided to shoot Mr Griffiths so that she might be hanged alongside Allen, her hero and the other Fenians. She refused to say anything more but it was believed that upon realising how well the barber was being protected, she decided instead, to shoot the constable and she was charged with his attempted murder. Her trial took place at the Manchester Winter Assizes on 4 December, at which she pleaded not guilty to the charge. She claimed to have bought the pistol to use at the celebrations of her sister's birthday on 5 November and had simply visited Griffiths' shop out of interest and had no intention of harming him. She claimed that when Constable Connell spoke to her, he did so in a most offensive manner and accused her of being a prostitute, an allegation the officer denied most strenuously when he gave his evidence.

The defendant explained that she was so enraged, she produced the pistol, but she wished only to frighten him. She denied telling him she wished to kill Griffiths in the hope that by so doing, she would hang alongside Allen. She acknowledged attempting to visit Allen but declined to give details of the nature of that relationship and suggested that if she wished to shoot anyone it would have been the prison officer who denied her entry to the gaol.

At the close of the evidence, the jury retired for one hour and on returning to the courtroom, the jury foreman told the judge, 'I am desired by the jury to recommend the prisoner to your mercy with all the emphasis which I am capable of.' The judge sought clarification by asking, 'Do you find her guilty of intent?' the foreman replied in the affirmative but a member of the jury shouted, 'Not of the intent.' The judge ordered the jury to retire and return with a unanimous verdict and twenty minutes later they did so, declaring she had indeed acted with intent.

The prisoner was sentenced to five years penal servitude and on learning her fate she shouted, 'Thank you my Lord, but I would have preferred to be hanged.' She was led out of the dock, shouting, 'Ireland, Ireland.' The apparent attitude of at least one of the jury reflected a widely held view that the accused was a naïve young woman who had no significant involvement with the Fenians and had acted alone. For instance, an editorial in the *Manchester Times* of 7 December included the following observations:

> 'We have a great horror of those crimes of violence which have now become only too common and we would punish their proved perpetrators with the utmost rigour. But the offence must in every instance be clearly established and no one should be convicted of a more serious crime than he has committed. In the present case we do not hesitate to say that the charge of attempted murder is hardly borne out by the facts. It is very foolish of any young woman to go about with a loaded, even though in this case, it may be an uncapped, pistol. Morally speaking it may be

assumed that she means mischief, but so long as she sins
only in intention, she cannot be punished for that.'

The events which led to Adelaide Macdonald's conviction had begun
three months earlier, in the early hours of 11 September, with the
arrests of two men on Oldham Street in Manchester. They were acting
suspiciously and were detained initially by officers who believed they
were about to break into a shop. However, they spoke with American
accents and as each of them was carrying a revolver, which neither
attempted to use, they were suspected of being Fenians.

Checks were made with members of the Irish police who were
stationed in Liverpool to assist in identifying members of the
nationalist organisation and confirmation was received that the two
prisoners were 36-year-old Colonel Thomas Kelly and 29-year-
old Captain Timothy Deasey. Kelly was a leading figure in the
organisation and Deasey acted as his assistant. Their detention was
authorised in Belle Vue Gaol until 18 September, on which date
Manchester would become the scene of one of the most sensational
crimes of the Victorian age. The Fenian movement had recruited
many Irish Americans in the mid-1860s, following the end of the
American civil war. Soldiers of Irish descent, who had fought on
both sides, found common cause and crossed the Atlantic to put their
military experience at the service of those seeking an independent
Ireland.

Earlier in 1867, there had been an attempted Fenian uprising in
Ireland, which had been crushed and the men detained in Manchester
were two of the many who had escaped to the mainland, intending to
reorganise. Kelly had in fact opposed the uprising as he considered
the organisation was ill-prepared. This had made him unpopular with
some of his comrades but his arrest was recognised to be a body blow
to the organisation, as he was known to be a brave man, excellent
organiser and a charismatic leader. His rescue would certainly improve
morale within the movement and be the cause of great embarrassment
to the British authorities.

Kelly and Deasey were visited in the gaol by a man who gave
his name as Edward Shore, who was described as a friend, who was
supposedly arranging legal representation for them. However, he
was in fact Edward O'Meagher Condon, the leader of the Fenians in

the North West of England, who was actually planning a spectacular rescue of the two men. He had realised that the van which transported prisoners between the gaol and the court building took the same route and made the journey at about the same time every day. He found what he believed to be the ideal location for such a rescue attempt, which was the railway arch on Hyde Road. Despite having only a few days to find the necessary weapons and men to participate in the rescue, he obtained guns from sympathisers in Birmingham and there were many men who volunteered from amongst Manchester's Irish community.

On 18 September Kelly and Deasey appeared at the city police court and at this hearing Inspector Adolphus Williamson of the Metropolitan Police, formally identified them. The inspector also confirmed that they were suspected of participating in the uprising in Ireland a few months earlier. He requested a further remand in custody for one week, which the court agreed to. They were placed in a cell to await the van, which at three o'clock was to return them and several other prisoners to the gaol. When the van arrived at the front of the court building, the police noticed two men acting suspiciously. Fearing they were Fenian sympathisers, several officers rushed towards them and although one escaped, the other drew out a knife with which he attempted to stab one of the officers. However, he was prevented from doing so and was arrested. This incident was not part of the planned rescue.

The prisoners were then led into the van and the handcuffed Kelly and Deasey were put in a separate compartment, thus segregating them from the other prisoners, who sat in the van's corridor with Police Sergeant Charles Brett, who was armed with his cutlass only. It was unusual for an officer to sit there and the sergeant was present in order that he might listen and report on any conversation the two Fenians had with each other.

The driver and the seven officers sitting on the outside of the van itself, together with four other officers following behind in a cab, were all unarmed as they set off on the three mile journey. This was incident free until it reached the railway arch and what happened next has been the subject of argument and debate ever since. The following account is based largely on details provided by a number of witnesses, although it should be remembered that their statements

The raid on the prison van. (The Illustrated Police News)

almost led to a serious miscarriage of justice, which could have led to an innocent man being hanged.

As the van was approaching the arch, a group of armed men, numbering at least twenty, moved towards the middle of the road. One of them fired his revolver into the air and another man shot the two horses, thus preventing the van from moving forward. The officers sitting on the van were forced to jump down and retreat a little distance which enabled the attackers to surround it without difficulty. Some of them climbed onto the roof, which they tried to break through, using a hammer, axe and stones, while others held at bay the police officers and a number of civilians who were attempting to help them.

One of the men put his revolver through the ventilator flap of the door and was heard to demand that the keys should be passed to him. After a few moments he was seen to fire his weapon into the van. The keys were passed to him and as he opened the door, the sergeant, who had suffered a serious head wound, fell out. Several women prisoners emerged screaming from the van and fled the scene. They were followed moments later by Kelly and Deasey, who made for the railway line, which was only a matter of yards away, guided by some of their rescuers. They were pursued unsuccessfully by a group of police officers and civilians. Several warders from

Belle Vue Gaol, who had been told of the attack by a cabman, arrived to offer assistance and although Kelly, Deasey and many of the rescuers managed to escape, a large number were captured on Hyde Road and the surrounding area.

Several people suffered gunshot wounds but the 51-year-old sergeant was the only fatality. Witness accounts suggest the rescuers apparently attempted to avoid unnecessary casualties and several experienced police officers believed that many of the weapons used by the Fenians contained blanks. Credence can be given to this belief when it is realised that those taking a leading role in the rescue did have loaded weapons but were taken into custody by unarmed officers and civilians, as when surrounded, they tended to fire into the ground or the air, in an attempt to frighten their captors rather than shoot at them directly.

Brett was popular with his colleagues and respected by the officials at the city police court, where he acted as the dock officer and where he had a reputation of treating the criminals in his charge with compassion and fairness. That he left a widow and three children added to the sense of sorrow felt throughout the city.

The first account of the rescue was given at the inquest into the sergeant's death. Constable George Shaw, who was sitting on top of the van, became the first witness to formally identify William Allen as the man who fired the shot which killed the sergeant. He recalled seeing Allen at the van door and firing several shots to warn people not to approach him. After shouting through the door, the witness said he took deliberate aim with his weapon at the ventilation flap and fire. A few moments later, he heard a woman's voice from inside the van, scream, 'He's shot!' The door opened and the sergeant fell out. A member of the coroner's jury asked the constable if he believed whoever fired the fatal shot, was aware there was a police officer inside, to which he replied that in his view he must have been.

The next witness was Mr John Woodcock, house surgeon at the Manchester Royal Infirmary, where the wounded officer was taken at four-thirty that afternoon. He had suffered a gunshot wound to his right eye and he died one hour later without regaining consciousness. A post-mortem revealed extensive injuries to the brain, which had been the cause of death.

A number of suspects were detained in the days that followed and a series of line-ups took place at the town hall. As a result, twenty-six men appeared at a Special Commission, which opened in Manchester on 28 October, before Mr Justice Mellor and Mt Justice Blackburn. This was despite defence lawyers arguing that it should be held in London as they believed feelings were running so high in Manchester that it would not be possible to find an unbiased jury.

At the conclusion of their trials, the following received varying sentences of penal servitude; John Carroll, Charles Moorhouse, John Brannon, Thomas Scalley, Timothy Featherstone, William Murphy and Daniel Radden. The following year, William Darragh would be convicted of obtaining in Birmingham the weapons used in the rescue. He was sentenced to death but was later reprieved.

Five of those being held were identified as having played leading roles in the planning and execution of the rescue and these were William O'Meara Allen (19), Michael Larkin (30), Thomas Maguire (31), William Gould (30) and Edward Shore (26). These were the names under which they were tried, but Gould had given his real name, which was Captain Michael O'Brien, adding he had served in the same regiment as Kelly during the American civil war. Shore's true identity would become known later.

To support its case against these five men the crown called several police officers to testify. Constable Joseph Yarwood, who was sitting with the driver, told the court he saw Larkin and Gould shoot the horses. He then saw Allen with a revolver in each hand at the van door. Constable Shaw identified Larkin, Gould and Shore, all of whom were armed, in the main group of attackers. Constable William Carrington told the court Allen had pointed two pistols at him, before shooting a civilian, Henry Sprosson in the foot. Detective Seth Bromley told of being shot in the thigh by Allen, who he later saw on the van roof attempting to force an entry. Other incriminating evidence against Shore and Gould was given by Constables Thomas and Truman.

A number of civilian witnesses were also called. Robert Patterson and George Pickup both saw Kelly and Deasey leave the van and heard Allen shout, 'Ah Kelly, I'll die for you before I deliver you up.' William Hulley, landlord of the nearby Railway Inn, stated that Allen had shot at him and his wife as they were standing in their doorway. Henry Sprosson worked at St Matthew's Church on Hyde Road and attempted to help the police. However, as he ran towards the van he heard another onlooker shout, 'Come back you fool,' and as he turned round, he felt a bullet enter his foot, but he had not seen who shot him.

It was now that John Griffiths entered the witness box to recall what he saw, which would lead to him becoming a marked man. He was in his shop and became aware that something unusual was clearly happening outside, so he raised his shutters and went to stand in his doorway. He noticed eight men at the arch, each of whom was carrying a revolver and as the van approached, they rushed towards it and began firing their weapons. The witness was joined by Henry Sprosson and they watched as Allen, a weapon in each hand, threaten anyone who attempted to hinder the rescuers and he clearly believed Henry had been about to do when he shot him in the foot. He then saw Allen at the van door fire into the ventilation flap, after which the sergeant fell out. Later, Mr Griffiths helped carry the sergeant to a cab in which the wounded officer was taken to the Infirmary. He also testified that he had not seen the defendant Maguire play any part in the rescue.

The prisoners inside the van, Emma Halliday, Ellen Cooper, Frances Armstrong and 12-year-old Joseph Parkinson, a juvenile offender, gave dramatic descriptions of the attack. They told of the van coming to a sudden halt, hearing the shots and the sound of stones being thrown against its sides and of the attempts to force entry through the roof. Not knowing what was happening added to their fear and the only individual to remain calm was Sergeant Brett. He had looked through the ventilation flap and exclaimed, 'Oh my God, it is those Fenians.'

They told of hearing a man's voice shout through the flap, 'If you give us the keys we will let the two men go and do you no harm.' The sergeant replied, 'Whatever happens, I will stick to my post to the last.' The man responded by screaming, 'Get me the keys or I'll blow your brains out!' A revolver was pushed through the flap and Emma grabbed at the sergeant's uniform and crying out, 'Oh Charlie, do come away,' attempted to pull him out of harm's way. There was a gunshot and the sergeant fell to the floor, mortally wounded. Emma insisted Allen was responsible as she could see him through the flap. The keys were passed to him and when the door opened the prisoners ran off.

The court was also provided with details of the arrests of those standing in the dock. Local grocer John Knowles took his revolver to join in the pursuit and exchanged fire with Allen. George Moorhouse grabbed Gould, telling him, 'My man, I think I've got you and be hanged.' This was despite being shot at by Allen who was then overpowered by a group of men, one of whom attempted to beat him about the head with one of his own revolvers, before he was handed over to the police. Joseph Howard, a prison warder, helped detain Larkin in the nearby railway goods yard, where he too was being assaulted by several men, before the warder took hold of him. Another warder John Baxter was able to detain Gould. Maguire and Shore were arrested some time later, away from Hyde Road.

The defence barristers did not cross examine the crown witnesses to any great extent, other than to highlight some discrepancies in the evidence presented. Instead, it was argued that the defendants should be charged with manslaughter rather than murder. It was claimed that the detention of Kelly and Deasey was wrongly authorised by the magistrates, meaning they were being held in custody illegally. If an individual so detained attempted to escape and in the process someone was killed, the charge should be the lesser one.

The judges retired to consider this argument and returned thirty minutes later. They believed there would perhaps be some merit in this claim if the individual who was illegally detained took the action described. However, this was not the case if others took it upon themselves to attempt to aid an escape and therefore, murder was the appropriate charge their clients should face.

This approach having failed, the defence called alibi witnesses on behalf of three of the accused. Mary Flanagan, a governess who claimed not to have known Gould previously, testified that she saw him outside a public house, some distance from Hyde Road at three fifty, which would have made it impossible for him to have participated in the rescue. Another witness, Mary O'Leary also spoke on behalf of Gould. Isabella Fee, a beerhouse keeper on Rochdale Road testified that Shore and been in her premises at the time of the rescue and she was supported by her son and another customer, Francis Kelly.

Several witnesses appeared on behalf of Maguire. He was a Royal Marine, on leave after serving overseas for many years, who following

Above left: Larkin, Allen and Gould. (The Illustrated Police News)

Above right: Larkin bids an emotional farewell to his mother, wife and children on the eve of his execution. (The Illustrated Police News)

his arrest said he did not know where Hyde Road was. He was staying with his sister, Elizabeth Fayden at her Salford home and she insisted he had not left the house until seven thirty that night, as he had been unwell and six of her neighbours testified they had spoken to him at various times during the day.

Nevertheless, the jury convicted him and the other defendants of Brett's murder and when asked if they had anything to say, all protested they were innocent, but they were sentenced to death. However, the members of the press who had been covering the trial, convinced of Maguire's innocence, immediately wrote to the Home Secretary, voicing their concerns and asked for a pardon. Despite fears expressed by some, that to agree to this unusual request would possibly undermine the case against the others, Maguire was pardoned and released. So, after spending a short time in the condemned cell, he was able to resume his career in the Royal Marines.

Furthermore, when Shore's true identity was revealed and it became known he was an American citizen, his government petitioned for a reprieve. This was agreed to and his sentence was commuted to life imprisonment. This led to hopes being raised that the three remaining prisoners might also be reprieved, but this did not happen and their executions were set for the morning of 23 November, outside the New Bailey Gaol in Salford.

The government feared the Fenians would mount another rescue attempt, this time of the three condemned men and anyone on the streets of Manchester and Salford on the eve of the hangings would have thought they were in an area under military occupation. The railway line near to the gaol was closed to traffic twenty-four hours before the executions were to take pace and a company of the 54th Regiment was camped nearby. Troops and Special Constables shared responsibility for guarding the space immediately in front of the scaffold. The sense of unease became almost tangible when it was learnt that William Calcraft had received the following anonymous letter:

The prisoners are pinioned prior to the executions. (The Illustrated Police News)

'Sir, if you hang any of the gentlemen condemned to death at the New Bailey Prison, it will be the worse for you. You will not survive afterwards.'

As the crowds began to gather at the scaffold, the condemned men were spending their last night with their priests. Larkin, the only married man, had said tearful farewells to his mother, wife and four children earlier in the day. Allen had been refused permission to see Mary Anne Hickey, the young woman he had hoped to marry.

The condemned men woke early on the morning they were to die, attended mass at five thirty and were pinioned as they prayed. Outside, at a few minutes to eight, troops appeared on the ramparts and on each side of the gallows, but hidden from public view, was a platform, on which soldiers armed with loaded rifles, were positioned. Minutes later, the prisoners, the governor of the gaol, the priests and other officials came into view. The three Fenians were led onto the drop to a mixture of cries of derision and shouts of support from among the many thousands who had come to watch the spectacle. Gould and Allen embraced before Calcraft placed the white hood over the heads of the three men. The hangman stepped backwards

The Fenians are hanged outside the walls of the New Bailey Gaol. (The Illustrated Police News)

and pulled the lever, causing the men to fall through the drop. He had used three different lengths of rope, the longest being for Allen, who died instantly. However, Gould and Larkin struggled for some minutes before becoming still. As was customary, the bodies were left hanging for one hour before being cut down.

In 1897, a memorial to Allen, Larkin and Gould was erected in the city's Moston Cemetery, the foundation stone being laid by James Stephens, the leader of the Fenians in the 1860s. The three men are still remembered by Manchester's Irish nationalists at an annual act of remembrance. Sergeant Brett was buried three miles away in Harpurhey Cemetery and his widow was awarded a pension for life from a grateful city.

After being taken out of the van, Kelly and Deasey made good their escape. They later travelled to America, where it is said Deasey died in the 1880s and Kelly died in the early years of the twentieth century after a career as a New York customs officer. Shore served eleven years in English gaols before being released, after which he returned to America.

Following the executions, the Fenians were buried within the grounds of the gaol, but that did not prevent their sympathisers from holding a funeral procession in their honour through the streets of Manchester several days later. (The Illustrated Police News)

7

Constable John Cruickshanks
Durham County Constabulary
1868

31-year-old David Paton was born in Dunse, Berwickshire, where he began his working life as a gardener. However, yearning for adventure, he joined the artillery of the Honourable East India Company, before being appointed governor of a prison in India, where he remained for two years. He returned home and joined the East Lothian and Haddingtonshire Constabulary from which he later resigned following his demotion from sergeant to constable. He joined the Roxburgh force, which he left after a relatively short time with a reference signed by his chief constable, highlighting his good character and the valuable service he had given.

He spent a brief time with the Berwickshire force before transferring to the Durham Constabulary in October 1867 and was based initially in Pittington before being moved to Sherburn six months later. He lived in the village with his wife and 6-year-old son and very quickly became a popular member of the small community. The events of Friday 1 May 1868 therefore came as a great shock to his colleagues and neighbours alike.

On that afternoon, he appeared before a disciplinary hearing at the force's headquarters in Durham, which was presided over by the chief constable, Colonel White. Paton had been reported for drinking in a public house at three in the morning some days earlier, meaning he was absent from his beat and thus not performing his duty. Although serious, this would not necessarily have resulted in his dismissal and indeed after the allegation had been thoroughly investigated he was cleared of any wrongdoing.

However, during the proceedings it emerged that he had been allowed to resign from his post in East Lothian for failing to carry out his duties properly and furthermore, despite the excellent character reference, he was dismissed by the chief constable of the Roxburgh force for a breach of discipline. Colonel White, therefore, had no option other than to summarily dismiss Paton. The Home Office had issued instructions that any police officer dismissed by one constabulary could not be re-employed by another. When advised of this, Paton appeared to accept the decision and there was no display of anger. He calmly folded his cape, saying he would leave it there and agreed to return the next day with his uniform and to collect the wages owing to him.

A colleague, Constable John Cruickshanks had made the complaint regarding his early morning drinking and having served with Paton in Scotland, it was he who also provided the information about his previous history of indiscipline. Cruickshanks left the hearing some minutes before Paton, who nevertheless caught up with him and as he appeared friendly and to bear no grudge, the two men set off walking home together.

Cruickshanks, a native of Grange in Banffshire, worked as a farm labourer when a youngster. He had first joined the East Lothian force, in which he served with Paton, before joining the Durham Constabulary in late 1866 and was posted to Pittington. However, he resigned to join the Edinburgh Police from which he transferred to become a detective with the North British Railway Company. However, in February 1868, he re-joined the Durham Police and was once again posted to Pittington, where he set up home with his family. It was acknowledged by his superior officers and colleagues that he was not acting maliciously against Paton but was simply attempting to maintain high standards of behaviour within the force, which he had always argued was necessary to build the trust of the public they served; he had certainly not expected nor intended his colleague to be dismissed.

As they walked home, the two men were joined by Constable William MacKay, who was unaware that Paton had lost his job and did not know of the role played in the affair by Cruickshanks. He noticed nothing unusual in the demeanour of either man. They arrived at the Durham and Sunderland branch line of the North Eastern Railway Company, along which Cruickshanks usually walked as it was a shortcut to his home in Pittington. However, Paton asked him to continue with him as far as Sherburn as there was something in his house that he wished to hand over to him. Cruickshanks agreed and the three men resumed their journey.

It was six in the evening when they arrived in Sherburn and Cruickshanks said he would wait outside for Paton to bring him the item he wished to give him. Mackay accompanied Paton inside, went into the kitchen and poured himself a glass of water. He heard raised voices and assumed Paton and his wife were arguing over some domestic matter but what Mackay did not realise was that Paton had taken a loaded revolver from a chest and despite his wife's pleas, had walked out of the house to confront Cruickshanks. It was still light and there were several witnesses to what occurred next, but despite this, the incident was over so quickly that it proved impossible for anyone to intervene.

Paton approached Cruickshanks, carrying the revolver in his right hand, concealed behind his back, which when close to him, he produced and shot him in the groin. The wounded man made for a nearby public house, the Earl of Durham Arms, pursued by his assailant. He was shot for a second time on reaching the doorway, this time in the hip. Although badly injured, Cruickshanks ran into

The murder. (The Illustrated Police News)

the taproom, in which he sought shelter behind an upturned wooden bench. As he watched Paton raise his weapon once again, he moaned, 'Oh dear, murder.' There was a third shot and the bullet entered between his fifth and sixth ribs, killing him instantly.

Satisfied his victim was dead, Paton calmly walked out of the public house and into the street. Here, he raised his right hand, in which he was carrying the revolver, put it to his head behind his right ear and fired. He fell to the ground, still alive but of course, seriously injured. He was carried into his own house and Cruickshanks's body was taken to an upstairs room in the Earl of Durham Arms. Local surgeon George Shaw confirmed Cruickshanks was dead and he realised Paton was beyond help and he died two hours later

The joint inquest into both deaths was held the next day at the Earl of Durham Arms, before coroner Crofton Maynard after the jury had viewed both corpses, still dressed in their police uniforms. It was Constable Mackay who produced the six-chambered revolver used in the killings, for the jury to inspect. Paton had purchased it in India and there was a great deal of unease in the room when the witness stated it was still loaded with two bullets. The coroner ordered that it be taken to pieces immediately, which the constable did and the hearing continued without further incident.

That this revolver was the weapon used was confirmed by George Shaw, who also gave details of the post-mortems he had carried out on both men. Several villagers, who had been on the street in which the shootings began and ended with Paton's suicide, also gave evidence. However, it was the evidence of Paton's wife, Jessie, that was eagerly anticipated. She stated that whilst serving in India, her husband had been kicked about the head by a horse but had apparently recovered fully and had exhibited no signs of disturbed behaviour since. Nevertheless, in the past few days he had become greatly distressed, was unable to sleep and was acting unusually. He had spoken to her of problems at work but had given no specific details. Also, he had begun reading extracts from the Bible, which was something he had never done in the past.

During the previous week he had threatened to blow his brains out, which caused her great concern because she knew he possessed the revolver, but she did not know where in the house it was kept. Furthermore, since the middle of the previous week, he had been carrying two razors in his pockets and when she became aware of this, she feared he was contemplating suicide. He had given her no indication whatsoever of any feelings of antagonism against Cruickshanks or any other individual. On his return home on the previous evening, she realised something was wrong when she saw him with the revolver in his hand. She pleaded with him to put it down but he refused and it was this exchange Mackay had heard and which he believed to have been a simple disagreement. She had been unable to prevent her husband from leaving the house and moments later, she heard the first gunshot.

At the conclusion of the evidence, the coroner addressed the jury and said that he was sure they would agree with him that Cruickshanks was murdered by Paton, who had then taken his own life. It would appear that he felt a great deal of resentment towards his victim, who he must have held responsible for his dismissal from the police. Mr Maynard then drew the jury's attention to the refusal of the Church of England to permit the burial of those who committed suicide in consecrated ground, unless they were insane at the time. He asked them was, 'Paton to have the burial of a Christian or be interred like a dog?' He emphasised that if they found him to have been temporarily insane at the time of the shootings, their verdict would allow him to have a Christian burial.

The coroner clearly wished Paton to have a decent burial, probably to spare his family further distress, but after an absence of one hour, the jury foreman, Benjamin Brown delivered the following verdict, 'Wilful murder against David Paton so far as the death of John Cruickshanks is concerned. As to Paton's own death, a verdict of suicide, but whether in a sane or insane state of mind when committed, there is not sufficient evidence to show.'

At the close of the inquest, Cruickshanks's body was taken from the public house to his home in Pittington, escorted by several police colleagues. His funeral was due to take place on the Monday, but decomposition of the body had set in so quickly that it became necessary for it to be brought forward twenty-four hours, meaning that sadly, many of his relatives in Scotland could not be present. Therefore, at three on that afternoon, his coffin was placed in a hearse, which made the short journey to the village church. Following behind, in a procession led by his 7-year-old son, were his family, friends, neighbours and a party of police officers. In line with custom in the district's mining villages, members of the local Primitive

Methodists accompanied the hearse and sang hymns along the route and at the graveside. Cruickshanks was buried on the south side of the graveyard and a plate on his coffin was inscribed with the words 'John Cruickshanks, died May 1st 1868 aged 30 years'.

The church did agree that Paton could be buried in the same graveyard as his victim the following day, but the event did not pass incident-free. His coffin was also accompanied by family, friends, two members of the Durham (Seaham) Artillery Volunteers and many neighbours who, despite the dead man's actions, wished to demonstrate their support for his widow. The Primitive Methodists were again present as were members of the Earl Vale Lodge of Oddfellows, of which he had been a member. They had hoped to read the funeral service of the Oddfellows, but following objections being raised by the vicar, the plan was abandoned.

8

Constable Richard Hill
Bristol Constabulary
1869

In early 1886, a petition was submitted to the Home Secretary seeking the release of William Pullin from prison. It was signed by twelve thousand residents of Bristol, including several clergymen and a number of the city's magistrates. Pullin had been convicted of murdering Police Constable Richard Hill of the local force, seventeen years earlier, when the killer was just nineteen years of age. He was due to hang but was reprieved and instead was sentenced to penal servitude for life, the jury having recommended mercy.

Many now believed he had served sufficient time in prison and that given his youth at the time of the crime and his subsequent exemplary behaviour during his sentence, that it was an appropriate time to release him. It was evident that he would be welcomed back in Bristol and that there were many prepared to offer him help and support. The editor of the *Western Daily Press* in reporting on the petition noted:

> 'It is to be hoped that those who are interesting themselves
> in the case will be successful in their considerate and
> humane efforts.'

Despite the considerable local support, the Home Secretary refused to agree to Pullin's release.

The crime of which he was convicted was committed on the night of Saturday 24 April 1869 in the St Philip's district of Bristol. At nine o'clock, baker William Curtis saw Pullin ill-treating a donkey, by beating it viciously with a stick. Mr Curtis remonstrated with him and demanded that he stop immediately. Pullin was annoyed at this interference and followed the baker into his shop on West Street and approached him in a menacing manner.

Mr Curtis walked out of his shop, saying he would go in search of a police officer. Pullin followed him as far as the Three Horseshoes, a public house, where he approached the baker and struck him three or four times, forcing him to the ground. As he rose to his feet, a man not wearing a uniform, caught hold of the attacker, saying, 'I shall take him in charge.' This was Police Constable Richard Hill, who although on duty, was in plain clothes, at the request of his inspector, who hoped this would make it easier for him to gather information on crimes in the planning stage.

However, a large group of people gathered at the scene and pushed the constable and his intended prisoner through the door of the public house and into the lounge, clearly intent on releasing Pullin, as Hill had by now revealed he was an on-duty police officer. Nevertheless, the struggle continued for ten minutes and the other men continued to punch and kick the officer. A customer, George Cole, ran to St Philip's police station to report the incident and several officers were sent to assist Hill.

On hearing the fracas, Joseph Osborne, the landlord, had rushed from behind the bar in another room to investigate and saw Pullin and the constable on the floor and he heard Hill say, 'My God, he's got a knife.' Several police officers entered and dragged Pullin off their colleague and as he stood up, the landlord's wife Mary noticed a great deal of blood on the floor, as Hill had been stabbed twice in the left leg. She urged him to sit down and gave him a glass of brandy.

Dr Thomas Davies, whose rooms were close to the pub, was sent for and arrived to find the wounded constable in an insensible state, unable to speak and losing a large amount of blood from the two wounds. The doctor realised the constable was beyond help and he died soon afterwards. His body was placed on a stretcher and carried to the police station. The dead officer was 31 years of age and single. He had initially served with the Glamorganshire Constabulary and joined the Bristol force five years earlier. A popular officer, he had been stationed in the St Philip's Division for the previous two years.

Pullin worked as a labourer at a saw mill on Redcross Street and was unknown to the police, to whom it did not appear that he

SHOCKING MURDER OF A POLICEMAN AT BRISTOL

The murder. (The Illustrated Police News)

had been drinking to excess, reinforcing their view that the killing was premeditated. Accordingly, he was charged with 'Wilfully and feloniously killing and slaying PC273 Richard Hill in the execution of his duty', to which the prisoner replied, 'Can you prove it?'

A search of the crime scene was made but no knife was discovered, nor was one found when his clothes were searched at the station. However, the next morning, Constable Robert Gayner was on patrol in Bragg's Lane and noticed a large clap knife on the ground and on which there appeared to be blood stains. He returned immediately to the police station and handed it to his superior officers. Bragg's Lane was on the route Pullin was taken following his arrest and it was believed he had discarded it without being seen and that the murder weapon was now in the possession of the police.

The inquest opened on the afternoon of the following Monday and now, the brash confident Pullin had been replaced by an anxious young man, sitting with head bowed and sobbing uncontrollably. The coroner opened proceedings by addressing the jury and explaining that the case they were about to hear differed from those involving an affray, during which, in a moment of excitement and loss of control, one person struck another from which death ensued. In this current matter, an on-duty police officer was attacked and died from his injuries. The law allowed leniency for those convicted of the first type of crime, but in cases where police officers were attacked and killed, the law drew a distinction between them and others. This was because officers were under the peculiar protection of the law and it was of great importance, both to the public and the officers themselves that they should be supported in the execution of their duty.

A post-mortem had been performed by Ralph Bernard, surgeon to the Bristol Police, who was assisted by Mr Davies. They found the two stab wounds to the left thigh, the upper one of which was the more serious. It was three and a half inches long and by inserting his finger, Mr Bernard discovered it was more than two inches deep. The femoral artery had been severed, as a result of which, the constable bled to death within a few minutes. The damaged part of the artery had been put in a bottle for the members of the jury to examine. The lower wound was described as a simple puncture, which would not have caused any significant harm. The medical experts said that the knife found in Bragg's Lane might possibly have been the murder weapon but they were unable to give a categorical assurance that it was.

It was at the inquest and at Pullin's appearance before the local bench, that the police provided details of their evidence against him. Witnesses were called who had heard him threaten to stab Constable Hill if he did not release him as they fought each other. Joseph Osborne also appeared and he swore that he had seen the prisoner stab the officer. The physical evidence comprised items of Pullin's clothing, including his trousers and stockings which were saturated in what was said to have been his victim's blood. A verdict of wilful murder led to the accused being sent to the high court for trial.

At the close of the inquest, the foreman of the jury advised the coroner that the members wished to donate their fees towards a monument to be erected at the dead officer's grave. Hill was buried with full honours on the Thursday following his death and it was reported that his colleagues had opened a fund for such a memorial. This was completed in September by Bristol statuary, Mr G. Wood and included a full sized representation of his cape, belt and helmet together with a scroll which bore the inscription:

> 'In memory of Richard Hill, police constable of this city, who was murdered while in the execution of his duty in Gloucester-lane, 24 April 1869 aged 31 years and was interred in Arno's-vale Cemetery This tablet was erected as a mark of esteem by his brother officers and inhabitants in this city. In the midst of life we are in death.'

Pullin pleaded not guilty when his trial opened at the Bristol Assizes. His barrister pointed out that no knife had been positively traced to his client and suggested that those claiming to have heard him threaten to use the knife or to have witnessed the actual stabbing, were not lying, but their statements could not be relied upon, as they were no doubt confused, given the nature of the disturbance they found themselves in at the time.

Both the prosecution and defence made it clear that they believed the case rested on whether the jury believed that the constable was justified in making the arrest and whether Pullin knew he was a police officer. In his defence, Pullin claimed he could not have known given the officer was not wearing his uniform. In his summing up, the judge advised the jury that it would be wholly unrealistic for a police officer to say in all the difficult situations he might meet, 'Take notice good people, I am a police officer.' It was enough that he was acting in the manner of a policeman and if the jury believed Pullin would have realised his victim was doing so, then a murder verdict was appropriate. However, if they had any doubts at all about this issue, the option of manslaughter was open to them.

The jury retired for almost three hours and retuned with a verdict of guilty to murder 'while infuriated by drink' and added a strong recommendation for mercy given his youth and previous good character. After being sentenced to death, Pullin said, 'I entertained no ill-will towards the police officer. However, I must do my best and may God have mercy on me and also my mother and two sisters.' The Home Secretary later accepted the jury's recommendation and Pullin was sentenced to penal servitude for life.

Nevertheless, as the petition of 1886 suggests, the time had been reached when the people of Bristol came to believe that Pullin should be released and despite this initial failure they continued with their efforts. In 1889, the Home Secretary, Hugh Childers, agreed to his release. On 10 August, Pullin walked out of prison a free man and arrived back in Bristol two days later, where a large crowd had gathered at the railway station to greet him.

The following day, an interview he gave to a reporter from the *Bristol Mercury* was published, in which he spoke of his life behind bars and expressed his remorse over Constable Hill's death. He concluded by saying, 'I shall never forget the kindness I have experienced from the Bristol people and I shall endeavour to show my gratitude for it by leading an honest, steady and useful career,' and he was true to his word. He settled in the city and married, but sadly his daughter died in childhood. He kept a respectable boarding house until his death on 25 February 1913.

By 2009, the headstone of Constable Hill's grave was in a very poor condition. A fund, organised by Pullin's great-great-great-niece was successful in raising the £1,100 necessary to have the repairs carried out.

Hugh Childers, the Home Secretary who agreed to Pullin's release from prison. (The author)

9

Constable William Perry
Cardiff City Police
1872

On the morning of 31 December 1872, Constables Perry and Phillips of the Cardiff City Police were given the task of taking a pauper lunatic to the local workhouse. They travelled there by cab, in which, after reaching the institution, Phillips returned to the police station, leaving his colleague to complete the necessary formalities with workhouse staff. These were completed by eleven o'clock, when Perry set off walking back to the station. He had not gone far when he was joined by a butcher known as John Jones, the name he had chosen to call himself when he arrived in Cardiff some time earlier from Wolverhampton, but his real name was Bernard Swan

The two men were seen by a number of people, all of whom believed they were on friendly terms as they made their way towards the turnpike gate. One of these was Leah Mainwaring, who knew the constable and they exchanged greetings. As they passed each other, she heard Jones refer to an incident some months earlier at the local market where he had a stall, when the constable had reported him for a misdemeanour. Perry replied that he was only performing his duty. She then heard Jones invite the officer for a drink as they approached the Westgate Hotel. Jones was a few steps ahead of Perry and as they reached the door, she saw him suddenly turn round and stab the constable in the chest.

Showing great courage, Leah ran to confront Jones, demanding he put down his knife, but he ignored her. She was aware that someone had gone to notify the police and a doctor, so decided to visit the woman she knew he was living with, Ann Hollingsworth, to ask her to come to the hotel in order that she might persuade him to calm down and hopefully avoid further bloodshed. However, Ann was drunk and in a highly distressed state and refused to accompany her. She told Leah, Jones had been beating her throughout the previous night, which had led a fellow lodger to lock her into a bedroom so he could not get at her.

Several members of staff and hotel guests witnessed what followed and provided details of these events after the fatally wounded constable staggered into the hotel and fell to the floor. He was followed by Jones, who, still brandishing the knife shouted, 'I have done for him and now I'll do for myself.'

He began to pace up and down in front of the bar, refusing repeated requests to surrender the weapon. He suddenly attempted to stab himself, but his coat and waistcoat prevented him from succeeding. He therefore, calmly removed these items of clothing and stabbed himself a number of times in the chest, before placing the knife on a small table at which he sat down and rested his head on his folded arms. He remained still for some minutes, but rose to his feet and lay on the floor, saying to those present in the room that he was fully aware of what he had done and added, 'Now I am going to die.'

Constable William Jones arrived and demanded to know from the prostrate Jones the whereabouts of the knife. Jones responded by screaming, 'Shut your mouth and let me alone, I will die as fast as I can.' The weapon, which was a butcher's knife with a seven inch long blade, had been seized by a witness, who handed it to the constable. Dr Grange now arrived and made arrangements for Jones to be taken to the infirmary. The doctor had realised Perry, who was lying in the entrance hall near to the door was beyond help. Nevertheless, Jones approached his colleague and friend to try to help him but found him foaming at the mouth. Jones called out his name but there was no response and he died seconds later.

The deceased was 36 years old and left his widow and one child. He had served in the Cardiff force since July 1865 and had a lengthy history of public service. He was previously a member of the Merthyr Division of the county force and prior to that served in the Royal Artillery and was a former member of the Glamorganshire Artillery Reserves. He was a keen gardener and the previous June had won first prize and five shillings for his fuchsias at the Cardiff Working Men's Flower Show.

His body was taken to the mortuary, where it was established that several attempts had been made to stab him in the left side. However, the one fatal wound had been struck with considerable force, the knife penetrating his topcoat, tunic, waistcoat and two shirts, before entering his chest and the post-mortem confirmed this had pierced his heart. The constable was well-known throughout the district and the esteem in which he was held became apparent on the day of his funeral. It was estimated that 40,000 lined the route from his home, Melrose Cottage in Canton to the cemetery at Adamstown. The cortege included twenty-five cabs carrying family and friends, behind which came members of the military organisations to which he had belonged and representatives of police forces from across Wales. As the coffin was being lowered into the ground a group of school children sang the hymn 'Shall we gather at the river'.

A fund to help the late constable's family was opened by Cardiff's town councillors and many small donations from individuals were soon received. At the conclusion of the inquest into his death, the coroner's jury donated their combined fees of £2. Hutchinson & Tayleure's Grand Circus and Palace of Varieties on St Mary Street, announced they would donate the takings from the show on 8 January to the fund. The acts included trapeze artists the Young England Brothers and renowned acrobats the De Castro Troupe. The evening was a great success and £30 was raised.

For some time before the murder, Jones had been heard threatening to stab Perry to death, which the deceased had not been made aware of. The motive for the killing soon became evident. In early 1872, Jones had a stall on the local market from which he was selling his meat products. To attract customers, he offered free drinks of beer and he also hired a man to ring a bell loudly and incessantly, much to the annoyance of the other stallholders and visitors to the market. Perry was sent to reason with him but Jones was unwilling to comply with a request to act more responsibly and his obstinacy led to the constable taking him to the police station, where he was detained. Jones was clearly unable to forget what he viewed as an insult. Constable Richard Harling did not hear Jones make a threat to take Perry's life but was told by him that it was a disgrace that a respectable businessman was treated in such a manner by a police officer.

Public Amusements.

HUTCHINSON & TAYLEURE'S

GRAND CIRCUS & PALACE OF VARIETIES,

ST. MARY-STREET, CARDIFF.

CROWDED, CROWDED, CROWDED!
The universal cry is, Where do all the People come from?
Success crowns every engagement !

TO-NIGHT (MONDAY), JANUARY 6th,

AND DURING THE WEEK,

Another Great and Unapproachable Galaxy of Stars and Novelties

IMPORTANT ANNOUNCEMENT!

WEDNESDAY NEXT, JANUARY 8TH,

A FASHIONABLE EVENING PERFORMANCE

Will be given in aid of the Fund now being raised for the

BENEFIT OF THE WIDOW AND CHILD OF
THE LATE WILLIAM PERRY,

POLICE OFFICER,

Who was cruelly deprived of life on Tuesday, December 31st.

TICKETS TO BE HAD EVERYWHERE.

Every Evening the Marvellous

YOUNG ENGLAND BROTHERS,

In their truly wondrous Mid-Air Flights, Somersaults,
&c., on the Flying Trapeze.

The Renowned

DE CASTRO TROUPE

OF MALE AND FEMALE ACROBATS.

In New Classical Feats.

THE RIGS OF MR. BRIGGS,

or, the Humours of a Jockey Club, by Mr. Boorn, senior,
and the whole Company. 3028

There was a great deal of sympathy for Perry's family and fund raising took many forms. (The author)

At the infirmary, Jones was found to have four self-inflicted knife wounds to his chest. He was under continuous police guard and on several occasions, he had to be prevented from removing his bandages and tearing open his wounds as he remained intent on ending his life. Nevertheless, as the days passed, he seemed to improve and it was thought he would survive. However, his condition worsened rapidly and a clergyman was called to his bedside to prepare him to meet his death. He died at seven-thirty on the morning of 8 January.

At the inquest into his death, Ann Hollingsworth described Jones as a violent drunkard who often experienced delusions and tended to blame others for his problems and failures. However, she had not heard him threaten Perry by name. In the weeks leading up to Christmas he had remained sober, as he had agreed to slaughter a great many pigs for local butchers. He was not permitted to perform this task in the yard at their lodgings, so had done so in the grounds of a house owned by a friend, Thomas Thornton. He confirmed that when carrying out this work, during those few weeks, Jones had drunk only coffee as he was intent on slaughtering the animals in a humane and efficient manner. When this task was completed, he immediately began drinking again and over the Christmas period was drunk most of the time.

Dr Sheen, who performed the post-mortem, advised the coroner that the fatal wound had penetrated the lung and the jury had no hesitation in finding that Jones had died at his own hands. At the conclusion of the inquest, the members of the jury donated their fees to the fund set up for the benefit of Mrs Perry.

10

Constable George Baker
Lancashire Constabulary
1873

By the early 1870s, the initial widespread hostility shown towards the new professional police forces that had been created across the country some years earlier had reduced considerably. Nevertheless, it was not unknown for difficulties to arise, especially in working class districts, if officers were thought to have acted in what was regarded to be a heavy-handed manner and one such incident occurred in Salford.

Pitch and toss was a gambling game with elements of both skill and chance, in which those taking part threw coins at a mark and the one whose coin was nearest to it, then had the opportunity of tossing the opponents' coins and winning those landing head up. It had long been popular but by the second half of the century, it was played mainly by youths, who gathered in large numbers in public places and acted in a rowdy anti-social manner, much to the annoyance of the emerging middle-class residents. It was for this reason that the police across the country attempted to stamp it out.

It had become a problem in the area surrounding Chapel Street in Salford and it was decided by the town's senior police officers that something needed to be done. Uniformed officers had proved to be largely ineffective, for as soon as they were seen approaching, the youths would simply run away. It was reasoned therefore that officers in plain clothes might prove more successful and on the afternoon of Saturday 30 August 1873, a group of officers out of uniform, headed towards Chapel Street. They had one specific task and that was to disrupt any games of pitch and toss they came across.

One of them was 23-year-old Constable George Baker, who the previous March, had left his hometown of Bedford, where he worked

A group of youths playing at pitch and toss. (The author)

as a butcher, to journey north to join the Salford police. He was a single man and was lodging at the Regent Road Police Station. He and his colleagues soon noticed a large crowd, comprising about one hundred and fifty men, women and children, on Yorkshire Street. It became clear their suspicions that they were watching a group of youngsters playing a game of pitch and toss proved to be correct.

Baker identified himself as a police officer and grabbed hold of one of the players, 12-year-old William Doyle, who put up a fierce resistance as the officer attempted to arrest him. The crowd had not dispersed and was becoming increasingly hostile. One man shouted that the lad should be released as he had not been gambling and tried to free him. Constable Edward Minogue told the man to leave immediately or he too would be arrested, before turning to assist in detaining the youth.

The crowd was by now extremely angry and two stones were thrown at the officers but missed. However, a third stone struck Baker on the left side of his head, knocking him to the ground. Minogue believed he saw the man he had warned moments earlier, throw it.

He was about to grab hold of him, but Baker, blood pouring from the wound, asked to be taken to a nearby chemist on Chapel Street for assistance, which is where the two constables went, still holding on to young William.

After his injury was dressed, the officers and their prisoner went to the police office at the town hall, where Baker remained on duty. A search began for the man who threw the third stone, which was responsible for his injuries and local man, 38-year-old James Farrer, a van driver, was taken into custody. When he was brought in to the town hall for questioning, Baker said, 'That is the man who hit me with the stone.' At seven o'clock that evening, the injured constable complained of feeling unwell and a cab took him to the surgery of Dr Stocks. Following treatment, he returned to his lodgings and took to his bed, but sadly died a few hours later at three o'clock on the Sunday morning.

Two witnesses had come forward, a young girl named Frances Faulkner and a clog maker , John Gill, who were prepared to support the police. Both acknowledged they had not seen Farrer throw the stone, but confirmed he was at the scene and after the third stone was thrown, they saw him move his arm quickly down his side. When charged with assaulting the constable, the suspect said, 'You are mistaken this time.' Later, when advised that Baker had died and he was charged with his murder, Farrer replied, 'I am innocent, I never threw the stone.'

The stone which hit the constable was ten inches long, six inches wide and two inches thick and not surprisingly had caused significant damage, which became known to Dr Stocks when he performed a post-mortem. There was just one relatively small external wound, but on removing the scalp, the doctor discovered a fracture to the left side of the skull and that a piece of bone had penetrated a major artery, which was the cause of death.

Baker was buried in Salford Cemetery on the Wednesday following his death and a large number of his colleagues provided an escort for the coffin. Many members of his family were present, including his brother, who was a sergeant with the 13th Regiment. His father was unable to attend as he suffered from serious mental health problems.

The inquest into the constable's death had opened at the Wellington Inn on Regent Road on the day before his funeral. The coroner's jury heard from Constable Minogue and the civilian witnesses, who described the events leading up to the fatal injury being caused. Dr Stocks gave details of his post-mortem findings, at the conclusion of which the coroner summed up. He advised the jury that if they were satisfied Farrer had been properly identified as the stone thrower, they could reach no conclusion other than that he was guilty of wilful murder.

However, Farrer was not present at the hearing and the coroner gave the jury the option of adjourning so the accused man could attend and be given the opportunity of presenting his version of events. The jury deliberated for a few minutes and asked for an adjournment, which the coroner agreed to do until the eleventh of the month. At that hearing, despite the views expressed once again by the coroner, three members of the jury refused to return a verdict of wilful murder against Farrer. This led the coroner to bind over the jury, in their own recognisance, to appear at the trial of the accused man at the next assizes.

The trial opened on 3 December at the Salford Hundred Assizes before trial judge, Mr Baron Pollock and the crown witnesses repeated

MURDER OF A BEDFORD MAN.—On Saturday, August 30, police-constable George Frederick Baker, who at the commencement of this year was in business as a butcher in Bedford, and joined the Salford police force in March, was conveying a youth to the Town-hall with another officer, when they were assailed by a crowd, and Baker was struck by a stone near the left temple. Death ensued from the injury early on Sunday morning. A man has been apprehended. Deceased was buried at Salford on Wednesday, being followed to the grave by the members of the police force and his relatives, including a brother who is a sergeant in the 13th Regiment. The father was formerly sergeant-major in the Beds. Militia, but for some years has unfortunately been affected in his mind.

The Bedfordshire Times & Independent reports the death of local man, George Baker. (The author)

the evidence they gave at the inquest. As Constable Minogue was explaining the reason for the officers being in plain clothes, the judge asked why it was necessary for such a course of action, to which the officer replied, 'We were detailed for special duty in plain clothes.' In a tone of voice bordering on the sarcastic, the judge asked, 'Do you call picking up a boy for playing pitch and toss in the street a special duty?' The constable continued, 'Yes, that was what we were detailed for, to look out for lads gambling.' The manner in which the judge sought clarification from the witness appears to have reflected some of the concern that had been expressed by many Salford residents regarding this particular use of police resources.

In his defence, Farrer called Henry Stanley of Barton Moss, who described himself as a gentleman of independent means. He had been present when Baker was struck by the stone, which he witnessed. He had turned round immediately to see where it had come from and he insisted the accused man, who was standing next to him, could not possibly have thrown it.

Later that afternoon, Farrer was acquitted and left the court a free man. Nobody else was ever charged with causing the death of Constable Baker.

11

Constable Nicholas Cock
Lancashire Constabulary
1876

Such was Charles Peace's notoriety, Sherlock Holmes referred to him as 'My old friend Charlie Peace' in Sir Arthur Conan Doyle's short story *The Adventures of the Illustrious Client*. Born in Sheffield on 14 May 1832, Peace turned to a life of crime in his youth and served prison sentences for burglary and other serious crimes.

In the summer of 1876, at Darnall in Sheffield, he became obsessed with a neighbour, Catherine Dyson and she eventually had to make it clear that she wished all contact with him to stop. Nevertheless, he continued to pester her, which led to Mrs Dyson and her husband Arthur, to move to Eccleshall. This did not deter Peace, however, who on 29 October shot and killed Arthur outside his home. The killer fled but was arrested two years later in October 1878. He was tried, convicted and sentenced to death for the crime the following February at the Leeds Winter Assizes.

An official police photograph of Charles Peace. (The author)

Once in the condemned cell of Armley Gaol in Leeds, he confirmed that he would not petition for a reprieve, realising it would be futile to do so and began

POLICE NOTICE,

AMENDED DESCRIPTION OF

CHARLES PEACE,

alias GEORGE PARKER, *alias* ALEXANDER MANN, *alias* PAGANINI,

WANTED FOR

MURDER

AT SHEFFIELD;

He is thin and slightly built, 46 years of age but looks 10 years older, 5 feet 4 or 5 inches high, grey (nearly white) hair, beard, and whiskers, (the whiskers were long when he committed the murder but may now be cut or shaved off), has lost one or more fingers off left hand, cut mark on back of each hand and one on forehead, walks with his legs rather wide apart. speaks somewhat peculiarly, as though his tongue was too large for his mouth, and is a great boaster.

He is a joiner or picture-frame maker, but occasionally cleans and repairs clocks and watches, and sometimes deals in oleographs, engravings, pictures, &c. Associates with loose women and has been twice in penal servitude for burglaries near Manchester. He has lived in Manchester, Salford, Liverpool, and Hull.

Be good enough to make vigilant enquiries and communicate with

MR. J. JACKSON,

Chief Constable.

CENTRAL POLICE OFFICES,
SHEFFIELD, DEC. 4th, 1876.

A wanted poster issued after the murder of Arthur Dyson. (The author)

to settle his affairs. He was no dullard and with Henry Brion had been developing a machine for raising sunken vessels, on which they hoped to take out a patent. After his conviction, rumours began to circulate implying Henry was also his partner in crime. He therefore contacted Peace to ask if he would issue a written statement to say this was not so. The condemned man readily agreed to this request.

Following the final visit of his wife Hannah, he wrote his will, in which he left all his possessions to her. This left one final matter to resolve and on 19 February, he met with Reverend Littlewood, vicar of Darnall and at this meeting, Peace confessed to having committed another murder for which an innocent man had been wrongly convicted.

The crime to which Peace was referring was the murder of Constable Nicholas Cock, as midnight approached, on the night of 1 August 1876 at Whalley Range, Manchester. Cock was twenty-two years of age and single. He was formerly a miner in Cornwall, but eight months earlier had moved to Manchester to join the Lancashire Constabulary. He was quite small and was known to his colleagues as the 'little bobby'.

On the night in question, Cock was patrolling his beat in Whalley Range and met James Simpson, who was making his way home. They chatted for a few minutes, before being joined by another officer, Constable James Beanland. When the men reached a road junction known as West Point, they separated, Mr Simpson continuing on his way home and Beanland carried on walking his

Constable
Nicholas Cock.
(The author)

beat, which meant Cock was now alone. Mr Simpson had walked no more than two hundred yards, when he heard two shots in rapid succession, which were immediately followed by what he recognised to be Constable Cock's voice screaming 'Murder'. He ran back to the junction and found the constable lying on the ground, bleeding from a chest wound.

Beanland and another colleague, Constable William Ewan, had also heard the shots, as had local resident William West, all of whom arrived at the scene at about the same time. The men tried desperately to stem the flow of blood and the wounded man was asked if he knew who had shot him, but he was unconscious and could not reply. Just then, two night-soil carts, driven by council employees Abraham Ellison and William Morrell were passing and they agreed to take the wounded man and the others to the surgery of Dr John Dill, which was nearby.

The doctor realised immediately there was nothing he could do and the constable died forty minutes later. Superintendent James Bent had arrived at the surgery ten minutes before Cock passed away and attempted to speak with him but he was still incapable of coherent speech and was unable to provide any details of his attacker. Nevertheless, the superintendent was confident he knew of three possible suspects. A post mortem, performed by Dr Dill revealed he had been hit by one bullet only, which had shattered the fourth rib, forcing part of it into the lungs, before lodging in the spine.

The Habron brothers, William (19), Frank (22) and John (24) were Irishmen who had worked for nurseryman Francis Deakin for the past seven years. They lived in an outhouse Mr Deakin had built for them in his grounds, close to where the shooting took place. They enjoyed a drink but were essentially men of good character, highly regarded by their employer, who would often leave them in charge of his business if he was ever absent.

The superintendent was aware of growing tension between the brothers and his dead officer, during the previous few weeks. This followed the constable warning William and John about their drunken behaviour and that they faced being summoned before the local magistrates if this continued. This led the brothers to make threats against Cock, which were heard by a number of people, including Eleanor Carter, the landlady of the Royal Oak beerhouse, where they

The property of the Habron brothers' employer, where they were arrested. (The Illustrated Police News)

were regular customers. The threats became even more menacing after the officer charged William and John with being drunk. John had said to her, 'The little bobby is going to summons us. If he does, we will make it hot for him, for he has no right to interfere with us. We were close to our own home and not interfering with anybody. If he does, by God, we'll finish him.' At about the same time, she was present when William raised his glass as though in a mock toast and say, 'If the little bobby gets his way, we'll finish him.' On the day before the shooting, the constable advised Superintendent Bent that as he was passing the nursery in the recent past, the three brothers were at work and jeered him as he walked by and he heard one of them threaten him with physical harm. However, he had insisted he was not afraid and would not be intimidated by them.

Within an hour of the officer's death, the superintendent led a number of officers to Mr Deakin's nursery. As they approached the outhouse they could see a lighted candle inside but as they drew nearer, it was extinguished. As far as the superintendent was concerned, that indicated that they had been awake and were only pretending to have been woken by his officers when they demanded entry. He ordered the brothers to get dressed in the clothes and boots they had been wearing earlier that evening. When they had done so he advised them they were being detained on suspicion of being responsible for killing Cock. John responded by saying, 'I was in bed at the time,' although the time of the killing had not been mentioned, which served to reinforce the superintendent's certainty of their guilt.

A search of their accommodation was made but no weapon was discovered. However, when the brothers arrived at Old Trafford Police Station, two percussion caps were found in William's waistcoat pocket, about which he claimed to have no knowledge. The waistcoat had been given to him by Mr Deakin and William insisted the caps must have already been in the pocket. Mr Deakin would later confirm that this was in all probability correct.

The night's work was not at an end, for the superintendent made his way back to the crime scene, where he had earlier noticed several footprints and decided to attempt to make some impressions of them, but only one produced a good result. This was one of a left boot and although the outside row of nails was indistinct, those towards the centre could be made out. There was one row of thirteen nails, two nails at the toe and three at the front. When compared with William's boot, as far as the superintendent was concerned there were enough similarities to convince him the impression taken at the scene of the shooting was that of the suspect's boot.

It had emerged during the night that Mr Simpson and Constable Beanland had noticed a man standing at West Point a few minutes before the shooting. He was described as being average size, wearing a brown jacket and a pot hat. Convinced he was William Habron, the superintendent asked Mr Simpson to attend the police station a few hours later to look at him, but he could not make a positive identification, as Beanland also failed to do later.

Gunsmith William Griffiths confirmed the fatal bullet was a .442, although an extensive search of the nursery and the surrounding area had not uncovered the murder weapon. However, Superintendent Bent was made aware of a suspicious incident at an ironmonger's shop in Manchester, the day before the murder, by shop assistant Daniel McClelland.

He and his colleague, John Henry Simpson, were in the shop, when an Irishman came in asking for cartridges, but seemed ignorant of what precisely he required. He was shown a box of cartridges, which cost 3s.6d, but the customer said he could not afford to pay that sum and asked if he could buy a few only. When told it would not be possible to break the seal of the box, he left the premises. The assistants were taken to see William, but both could only say he might possibly have been the man. William denied in the strongest terms that it was him and he had never visited the shop. Nevertheless, the superintendent was convinced William had done so and although no cartridges were purchased, he believed it demonstrated that the murder was being planned by the brothers.

The dead officer was buried on the afternoon of the following Saturday. The cortege, which included his only relative, a sister, left Old Trafford Police Station at three o'clock. It was headed by the police band, behind which came delegations from the Manchester, Salford, Rochdale, Bury and Bolton forces. Many thousands of people lined the route to the parish church of Chorlton-cum-Hardy to pay their respects.

The crown acknowledged its case was largely circumstantial but insisted there was sufficient evidence against the three accused and this was presented at the inquest into the constable's death and at the committal hearing before the city's magistrates. There was the similarity of William's boot to that found at the murder scene and although the other impressions were less distinct, it was suggested that some of their features were similar to those on John's boots. No murder weapon had been discovered but it was argued that the police had been able to show that William had attempted to purchase cartridges, which confirmed the murder was premeditated.

Furthermore, the Habrons lived close to where Cock was shot and could have easily made their way back to the outhouse before anyone returned to the spot after hearing the shots.

The threats made by the brothers, some of which were made only hours before the murder and which had been heard by a number of people, were highlighted. It was recognised they arose from arguably minor matters, but the brothers clearly felt greatly aggrieved by the victim's behaviour towards them and this provided the motive for the crime. However, at the inquest, the coroner, in his concluding remarks made it clear that he believed there was insufficient evidence against Frank, who he believed to have been in bed at the time, as he had claimed since his arrest. The jury agreed and the crown decided not to pursue the case against him and only William and John were committed by the local bench to stand trial.

This opened at the Manchester Assizes on 27 November and the brothers' defence was presented. It was pointed out that no murder weapon had been discovered to link them to the crime and their employer had confirmed the percussion caps found in William's waistcoat were probably his. As for the claim that William

The Manchester Assize Courts, at which William Habron was convicted of murdering Constable Cock. (The Illustrated Police News)

attempted to buy some cartridges, which he denied, the assistants in the ironmonger's had not positively identified him. Furthermore, nobody had been able to confirm the stranger seen in the vicinity of the crime was William, as the crown was implying.

It was also argued that there were differences in the boot print said to be similar to William's and that none of the other impressions bore any resemblance to those worn by John. If the jury was persuaded there were sufficient grounds to believe the impressions had been left by one or more of the Habron brothers, no

Superintendent James Bent.
(The author)

evidence had been presented by the crown to confirm when they had been made, so they could have been there for some time before the murder took place.

It was acknowledged that the defendants had uttered threats against the deceased, but these were empty threats, which they had no intention of carrying out. Attention was drawn to the previous good characters of the accused and how highly they were regarded by their employer, Mr Deakin. Their barrister poured scorn on the notion that being charged with drunkenness provided a motive for such a serious crime. Witnesses were also called who provided alibis for the two accused, who were said to be drinking in the Lloyd's Hotel and Royal Oak at the time of the shooting

The jury was absent for two and a half hours before returning with a not guilty verdict in respect of John but one of guilty against William, to which a strong recommendation for mercy due to his youth was added. After being sentenced to death he turned to the jury and judge and in a faint voice said, 'I am innocent of it.' He was removed from the dock to be taken to the condemned cell in Strangeways Gaol.

The press coverage of the trial and conviction contained some concern regarding the reliability of circumstantial evidence, which prompted the following letter, written by a member of the jury, to the editor of the *Manchester Courier*:

> 'Sir, - On your leader of today on the trial of John and William Habron, if not out of place, I should like to say a word or two about the matter. You say, referring to the jury, "They of course give no reasons for their decision. In all probability they have been greatly influenced by the discovery of the footprint and the inquiry about the cartridges". I think I may say the jury were immensely influenced by the footprint, as in the course of the evidence and the address of the counsel and also in the summing up of the judge, it came out strongly that the footprint was exactly like William's boot and that there were such peculiarities about the boot as to lead one to think it all but impossible there could be another like it; this, coupled with all the other details in the case, led almost at once, ten of the jury to a verdict of guilty so far as William was concerned, but with a strong recommendation for mercy. Eventually, all agreed the verdict and it will be the greatest satisfaction to all the jury if the recommendation to mercy is acted upon. I am &c, ONE OF THE JURY, November 29, 1876.'

Widespread concern continued to be expressed as indicated in this letter which appeared in the Courier a few days later:

> 'Sir, - Ever since the condemnation of William Habron, I have been hoping that someone of greater influence than myself would take up his case. I do not know what may be the general opinion of the verdict, but I find several friends feeling with me and feeling strongly, that the verdict was not justified by the evidence. It seems to me that the evidence, as indeed shown in the summing up of the learned judge, amounted, at the utmost, to a grave suspicion. Can nothing, then, be done to avert a fate so awful from a very possibly innocent man –one too only

eighteen? Yours &c, R HENRY GIBSON, BA, Parsonage Road, Withington. December 2, 1876.'

A number of meetings were held locally which were attended by many concerned individuals, seeking a reprieve and a petition signed by four thousand Mancunians was forwarded to the Home Office. On 19 December, notification reached Manchester that the condemned man had been reprieved and William Habron began his sentence of life imprisonment, still protesting his innocence.

Nevertheless, despite the misgivings of many about the handling of the case and doubts concerning the verdict, Superintendent Bent was thanked for his role at the Lancashire Annual Sessions held in Preston on 28 December, at which, the following was passed:

'Resolved, that special acknowledgement be, and is hereby unanimously made of the prompt, vigorous and decisive action taken by Superintendent Bent in apprehending John and William Habron, suspected of having murdered P.C. Cock at Whalley Range on the 2nd of August last and of the remarkable skill, perseverance and judgement manifested by him in the collection of circumstantial evidence, by the means of which William Habron was convicted of murder at the assizes held at Manchester on the 28th day of November 1876.'

Following the introduction of the Capital Punishment Amendment Act of 1868, which put an end to public executions, hangings now took place in private, behind prison walls. However, on the morning of 25 February 1879, despite a heavy fall of snow, a large crowd had gathered outside the gates of Armley Gaol. Inside, Peace was woken at a quarter to six and ate a breakfast of eggs, bacon and toast, which was followed by a large mug of tea. Later, William Marwood, the hangman, entered the cell and the two men shook hands. The prisoner's arms were pinioned and he was led out onto the landing to join a procession of warders and officials, which included the governor, surgeon and chaplain. Led by the Under-Sheriff, who was carrying his rod of office, they made their way to the scaffold which was in an outside yard.

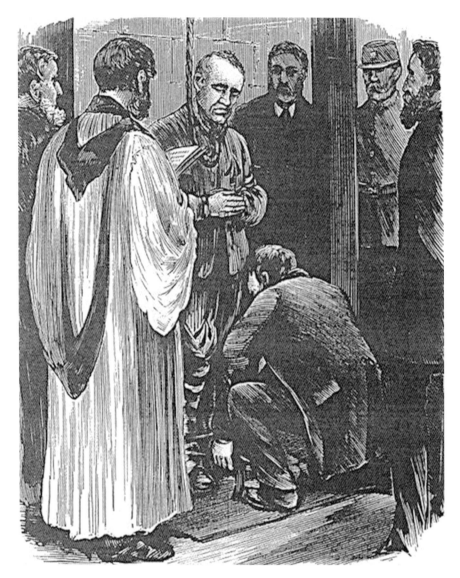

Peace stands on the gallows, awaiting execution. (The author)

Peace quickly climbed the twelve steps unaided and stood on the trap. Marwood tied his feet, but before the white cap was pulled down over his face, the governor allowed him to address the four journalists who had been granted permission to attend the execution. He told them his thoughts were with his children and he was sure the Lord would forgive his many sins; he concluded by saying, 'And now to

Above left: The inquest into Peace's death was held in the gaol. (The Illustrated Police News)

Above right: Peace was buried within the walls of the gaol. (The Illustrated Police News)

one and all, goodbye, goodbye.' He asked for a drink of water but this final request was refused. The white cap was pulled over his face, Marwood stepped back, pulled the lever and Peace fell into the pit, dying instantly. Three hours later, an inquest was held in the gaol in front of the local coroner. The cause of death was given and the jury decided Peace had been lawfully executed. The formalities at an end, he was buried within the gaol's walls shortly afterwards.

It was known that Peace had attended a great deal of the Habron brothers' trial so knew a great deal about the murder. This led many to believe he used the knowledge gained to give credence to his confession which was probably false, so as to delay his

I SAW MR DEAKIN AND KNEW THAT I WAS FREE

William Habron is greeted by Mr Deakin. (The Illustrated Police News)

execution. Nevertheless, despite initial scepticism, the authorities became convinced his confession was genuine. He had told of travelling to Whalley Range, intending to burgle several of the district's mansions and was confronted by Constable Cock. Peace produced a pistol and fired a warning shot, but this did not deter the officer, who attempted to detain him and it was then, that the fatal shot was fired.

Later, William who was serving his sentence at Portland, was taken to London's Millbank Prison, but he only became aware he was to be released when he was greeted there by his brothers and Mr Deakin, who had stood by him throughout his ordeal, convinced

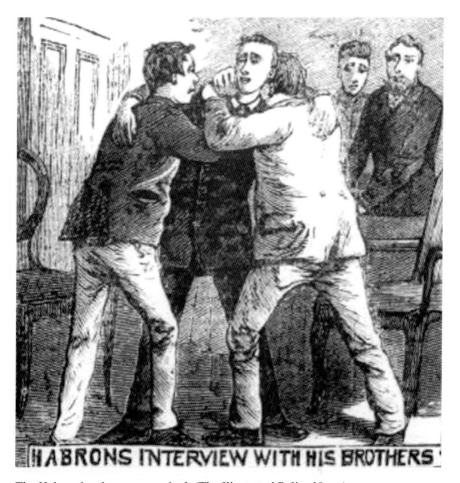

'HABRONS INTERVIEW WITH HIS BROTHERS'

The Habron brothers are reunited. (The Illustrated Police News)

of his innocence. He walked out of prison, a free man, on 18 March and later received compensation of £1000. He returned to live in Ireland but some years later made a brief tour of England, telling of his experiences, to raise funds for Irish charities. The tour proved to be a success and he was greeted with a great deal of warmth at all of the venues.

12

Constable John Menhinick
Lancashire Constabulary
1876

Holcombe is a village situated on the hillside above Ramsbottom, a few miles from Bury in Lancashire, which on the night of 29 July 1876, was the scene of a violent disturbance. It began in the Shoulder of Mutton public house and involved a number of Irish men and women who were living in the area. Constable John Menhinick was made aware of this and was the first police officer to arrive at the pub, just as those involved spilled out into the street. One of them, James Kerwin, who was extremely drunk, immediately began to assault the constable, who was forced to the ground. Two other constables, Markham and McLean arrived shortly afterwards, but the violence continued unabated.

Kerwin continued to resist all attempts to arrest him and he was assisted by Michael Duffy, with whom he lodged and his friends Michael Dolan, Michael Moon and Catherine Madden. The officers called out to members of the public, who were passing by to help them. John Domson and Charles Trillo responded, only for the latter to be hit twice in the face by Madden. Eventually, all of the offenders were detained and were subsequently brought up before the Bury Petty Sessions at which Duffy, Dolan, Moon and Madden were each fined ten shillings. The case against Kerwin could not proceed as Menhinick had not fully recovered from his injuries and the accused was remanded in custody until Monday 9 August.

When Kerwin finally appeared before the bench, details of just how vicious his kick to the constable's abdomen had been, became clear and the court was advised that he had not yet made a full recovery. The presiding magistrate, Mr T.L. Openshaw, read out details of the prisoner's past convictions, which included his four court appearances for violent offences. He was fined one shilling for causing criminal damage to Constable McLean's trousers and ten shillings in costs towards their repair. For the assault on Constable Menhinick, he was sentenced to six months imprisonment with hard labour. The injured officer was off work for two weeks before he was able to resume full duties.

On 12 September, Richard Wild, a senior magistrate for the district of South West Lancashire, died suddenly at his Birkdale home. A native of Bury, he had made arrangements to be buried at St Andrew's Church, Ramsbottom, where his funeral took place three days after his death. The police decided to send a group of officers to demonstrate the force's respect for him and Menhinick was one of those selected to attend. However, he collapsed and died shortly after the service ended and details were provided at the inquest into his death. This took place at the White Hart Inn, Holcombe on 18 September, before deputy-coroner, Mr J Makinson, who was determined to discover if the injuries caused by Kerwin had played any part in the constable's death.

The hearing opened with details of Menhinick's career and his family. The deceased was 33 years old and a native of London. He served in the 93rd Highlanders for ten years until May 1870 and joined the Bury Police in September 1873, having been working previously as a flax spinner in Aberdeen. Since joining the force, he had made steady progress, becoming a constable second class in April 1874, before rising to the rank of first class six months later. He left a widow, two sons and a daughter.

The first witness to appear was the late constable's widow, Isabella, who described the effect of the assault by Kerwin on her husband. He had told her that he was kicked with such force and felt so much pain, that he was convinced at the time that he would die immediately. During the two weeks he was off work, he complained repeatedly of a pain in the upper part of his stomach and to his back, which he injured when he fell to the ground. She applied warm cloths to both parts of his body but did not notice any bruises or other external signs of injury as she was doing so. He also told her that the left side of his body was painful and that he

The Old Dun Horse, where Constable Menhinick collapsed. (The author)

could not lie on it and although he returned to work, the discomfort continued. As he prepared to go on duty on the morning of the day he died, he told her the pain seemed to be worsening and that he was beginning to doubt if he would be able to continue to perform the duties of a police officer. Nevertheless, he was determined to attend Mr Wild's funeral and it was four o'clock that same afternoon that she was advised of his death and his corpse was brought to their house.

Menhinick's colleague and good friend Constable George Robinson told of visiting him at home following the assault and noticing how much he was suffering. The witness continued by stating that when he resumed his duties, he still did not look to have fully recovered. Following Mr Wild's funeral, he and Menhinick together with several other mourners visited the Old Dun Horse Inn in Ramsbottom, arriving at about two o'clock. They sat down to a meal, which they all enjoyed and drank several glasses of beer. They made their way to another room, in which Menhinick sat on a bench and lit a cigar. It was a few minutes later that he slumped to the floor, apparently unconscious. Surgeon James Smith, who lived close by, was asked to attend and was there within two minutes.

Constable Menhinick was buried in the graveyard of Emmanuel Church at Holcombe. (The author)

Constable Menhinick's grave.
(Claire Baggoley)

James Smith was the next witness to be called and he began by confirming there was nothing he could do for Menhinick, who died shortly after he arrived at the pub, without having regained consciousness. He then advised the hearing that he saw no external signs of violence to the body, before giving details of the post mortem he performed later. The skull was undamaged and so was the brain, except for a small partially absorbed clot of blood, which could not possibly have contributed to the officer's death. As for the heart, there was a rupture to the left auricle, the walls of which were thin and diseased. The liver was enlarged but essentially quite healthy. The stomach was in a very good state and contained the undigested remains of the meal he had just eaten. The witness emphasised that there were no signs of damage being caused by violence and that in his opinion he died due to pressure by a full stomach on a diseased heart, causing it to rupture. The damage to the heart must have been present for some considerable time and when questioned by the deputy coroner, the doctor was adamant that external violence such as that suffered at the hands of Kerwin could not have been responsible for the constable's death.

In his summing up of the evidence, Mr Makinson agreed with the surgeon's findings and believed the jury would be justified in finding that death was due to natural causes. This was the verdict reached by the jury and Kerwin faced no further action over the constable's death.

Constable John Menhinick was buried the following afternoon in the graveyard of Emmanuel Church, Holcombe. Family and friends were joined by twenty-two police officers and four former comrades who had served with him in the army. The funeral was also attended by many residents of Holcombe and Ramsbottom, by whom the dead officer was much respected.

As 1876 drew to a close, the County Constabulary Committee met in December and awarded Isabella Menhinick a gratuity of £16 10 shillings, the amount of one month's pay for each year's service, making a total of £49 10 shillings. She returned to her hometown of Aberdeen, where she remarried in 1879 and where she died five years later.

13

Inspector Joseph Drewitt & Constable Thomas Shorter
Berkshire Constabulary
1876

For much of the nineteenth century, poaching was a major problem in the British countryside. There were frequent violent confrontations involving poachers, gamekeepers and the police, which resulted in many deaths. As the century was drawing to a close, there was a marked decline in the crime, as the conditions of the agricultural workers and their families began to improve. However, the events in Berkshire in late 1876 demonstrate that the nation's rural districts still held many dangers.

On the night of Monday 11 December, Constable William Isaacs was patrolling his beat in Hungerford town centre and met Inspector Joseph Drewitt, head of the local force. They spoke for a few minutes before parting and the inspector advised his colleague that he was on his way to Denford Lane Toll Bar, where he had arranged to meet Constable Thomas Shorter. This was a local 'conference' or 'visiting' point, a mile or so out of the town, where officers could meet at set times to exchange information or receive instructions from superior officers. One path, known as Gypsy Lane, led from the toll bar into the Chilton Lodge Estate and another to Folly Farm. Nearby, there were two small cottages known as Picket Lot and the area was surrounded by fields. The officers parted at ten minutes after ten and it was twenty minutes later that the constable heard the sound of gunfire in the distance, but at the time, thought nothing more of it.

Constable William Golby came on duty at ten o'clock and as Inspector Drewitt was not in the station, he walked into Hungerford

Inspector Joseph Drewitt. (The author)

in search of him, to receive his instructions for the night. However, there was no sign of him and it was now ten forty-five. The constable decided to visit the Denford Lane Toll Bar and as he drew closer, he noticed what at first he believed to be a drunk, lying face down in the road. He tried unsuccessfully to rouse him, so grabbed hold of the man's collar. He felt something wet and on striking a match, he could see it was blood. It was only on lighting his lamp that he realised it was a policeman. He was now also able to see that his skull had been shattered and the large quantity of blood and fragments of brain indicated he must be dead. He did not turn the body over at this stage so did not know who the dead officer was.

Before returning to Hungerford for assistance, Colby called at the cottage of the gatekeeper, William Hedges and explained what had occurred. He asked him to keep watch for anyone who might be in the vicinity. The constable returned a short time later with colleagues and it was established that the dead officer was 24-year-old Shorter, who had been stationed at West Shefford. It was some time later, that a second body was discovered, which was that of 41-year-old Inspector Drewitt. He too was lying face down in a hedge row and had also suffered extensive head injuries. The truncheons of both officers were still in their pockets, which confirmed they did not have time to take them out to defend themselves and that they must have been taken by surprise.

On learning of the murders, Colonel Adam Blandy, the Chief Constable of the Berkshire Constabulary was soon at the scene and organised the gathering of evidence throughout the night. William Hedges told the police that five minutes after Golby left him, two local men, both of whom he knew well, passed by his cottage. They were William Day and William Tidbury, with whom he exchanged a few words before wishing them 'good night' and watched as they continued walking in the direction of their own home. Elizabeth Bryant, who lived in one of the cottages at Picket Lot, advised officers that at around ten thirty she heard men's voices outside and believed she recognised one of them as being that of William Tidbury. She, like Mr Hedges had not seen either man carrying a weapon of any kind.

The colonel ordered that a thorough search should be made of the crime scene and the surrounding fields for physical evidence, but even before this was completed, he believed there were sufficient grounds to arrest 39-year-old Day and 24-year-old William Tidbury. They lived in a shared cottage in the village of Eddington, as Tidbury was married to Day's daughter. The chief constable also gave instructions that the two other Tidbury brothers, Henry, who was 26, and 17-year-old Francis, should be detained. All four were well known poachers, although Francis had no criminal record. Later that morning the four suspects were arrested on suspicion of murdering the two officers, Day as he sat down to breakfast and the three brothers as they made their way to work at Cottrell's Iron Works at Eddington. All denied being involved in the killings.

Constable Thomas Shorter. (The author)

As the search for evidence continued, the broken lock of a gun was discovered under the constable's body, which it was believed must have come loose during the assault. It did not match the indentations to the constable's helmet and priority was given to finding the weapon's stock and barrel. An extensive search was made of Day's property and the stocks and barrels of two guns were found hidden in the grounds together with an axe handle.

The stock and barrel of one of the guns matched the indentations in Constable Shorter's helmet, convincing the police it had been used in his murder. The parts of the other gun could not be linked directly to the crimes. However, it became known that they were part of a gun sold by the Tidbury brothers to a workmate at the foundry, who put it in his locker for safekeeping. Shortly afterwards it was stolen and the Tidburys were suspected of being responsible and having it with them at the time of the killings.

Another important piece of evidence was found under the inspector's body and that was a man's cap. John Hancock, a foreman at Cotterell's, identified it as belonging to Henry Tidbury and was able to do so because of a distinctive button on its side. Tidbury wore it every day at work and had done so on the day of the murder. However, the police knew that it was no longer in his possession and when arrested he was wearing a black billycock hat. A tobacco-box, similar to one owned by Day was found close to the bodies, but it would not prove possible to link it with the suspect.

The nature and extent of the injuries sustained by the victims meant that those responsible must have been covered in blood and accordingly the clothes of the four suspects were examined. On all of these there was a great deal of blood, which was also found on the gun parts and axe handle discovered on Day's property. The police were satisfied that this was more evidence linking the four men to the murders.

The ground was soft the night the officers died and there were many footprints close to the bodies and in the surrounding area. Colonel Blandy arranged to have casts made of them and this was done with the assistance of a moulder from Cotterell's. Several proved to be quite distinctive and some similarities were found when they were compared with the boots of the men in custody. For instance, part of the heel of Henry Tidbury's right boot was missing and large nails had been used to make some earlier repairs and this matched one of the casts. The type of nails used on the outside of the heel of the boots belonging to his brother Francis, were similar to those on another of the casts.

The truly horrific nature of the injuries sustained by the two officers became apparent when Doctor Major, who performed post-mortems on both men, reported his findings at the inquest into their deaths, held at the town's John O'Gaunt Inn. They were attacked from behind, meaning their faces were intact and recognisable, but they had suffered catastrophic injuries to the backs of their heads and the damage to their brains had been the cause of death in both cases. There were no injuries to the lower part of the inspector's body but there was a gunshot wound to the right side of his neck. Burn marks to the collar of his uniform indicated he was shot at extremely close range and forty pieces of shot were extracted from his head and upper body. His death had been instantaneous, but the constable had taken longer to die. There were no gunshot injuries but there was a large amount of bruising to the whole of his body and several bones were broken, leading the doctor to conclude he had been beaten to death. The massive damage to his skull was caused by a blunt instrument, such as the butt of a rifle.

The two officers were buried with full honours a few days after the inquest. The constable left a widow and the inspector a widow and five children, the eldest of whom was just eleven years old. In the days leading up to the murders, the inspector had organised a collection at the police station for the family of Constable Nathaniel Cox, who was murdered in Yeovil, Somerset on 16 November by a gang of poachers. The descriptions of the wanted men were circulated to forces in the south of the country. On their arrival at Hungerford, the inspector took a handbill to be displayed by Mr Davis, the local stationmaster, who later recalled the officer say 'I don't think there are any people about here, bad enough to commit such a deed'.

Ironically, the *Reading Mercury* published the following letter a short time later:

> 'Sir, I have reason to think that very many are anxious to show their hearty approbation of the services of the late Inspector Drewitt for eighteen years in the Berks constabulary and their sympathy with those who have been laid low in affliction by his and P.C. Shorter's sudden and violent death. I have therefore suggested that a subscription should be opened on behalf of the sufferers

and I hope that such an amount may be collected as will secure for them some permanent benefit.

'The county magistrates will, no doubt, liberally exercise the powers vested in them by Act of Parliament, but these powers are limited.

'There might be a difficulty in appointing a committee of the subscribers to decide upon the application of the funds collected. I would therefore suggest that Colonel Blandy, the Chief Constable and the Police Committee should be entrusted with that duty and that any subscriber shall appropriate his donation, if he pleases, to either Inspector Drewitt's widow and children or to P.C. Shorter's widow.

'Subscriptions will be received by Messrs. Stephens & Co. and Messrs. Simonds & Co., Reading; by Messrs. Bunny & Co., Newbury; and by Colonel Blandy.

'I am Sir, yours faithfully,

'RICHARD BENYON, Englefield House, December 21, 1876'

Within a very short time, in excess of £200 was raised and donations continued to be sent for some time afterwards. Well-wishers also opened a fund for Constable Golby in appreciation of his professionalism, which, it was believed, had contributed greatly to the early capture of the perpetrators.

Colonel Blandy was confident that the physical evidence discovered at the scene, the information provided by Elizabeth Bryant and William Hedges and the results of the post-mortems, meant that it was possible to reconstruct the events of the night of the murders. The suspects were probably on their way home and their footprints showed they emerged from property owned by Mr Cherry, walked through a turnip field on Folly Farm and passed Picket Lot, heading for the toll-bar, where the deadly confrontation occurred.

It was thought that they were seen by the two officers and the inspector may have grabbed hold of one of them and was shot immediately in the back of the neck by one of the others. On seeing this, the constable attempted to run away but was chased and when the men caught up with him, he was felled to the ground with the butt of a gun. This was done with such force that the weapon broke into pieces. He was then kicked and beaten so severely that his skull was fractured in many places and parts of his brain were scattered across the immediate area.

The trial of the four accused opened at the Berkshire Lent Assizes on 19 February 1877 and lasted for two days. In line with custom, they were charged with one murder only, that of Constable Shorter. Day and William Tidbury were represented by a different barrister from the other defendants and all entered not guilty pleas. From the start, the crown admitted that the evidence against all the men was circumstantial and that it was not possible to say the blood found on their clothes and other items was human, nor could it be shown when the footprints at the scene were made.

Day and William agreed they were in the vicinity on the night of the murders but insisted they were repairing a piece of machinery belonging to local farmer, Mr Piggott. This was confirmed by the farmer and his servants, all of whom stated that the pair had worked between eight and ten o'clock. They recalled walking home and had seen what they now realise was the constable's corpse, but believing in the darkness that it was a drunk, had walked on without offering assistance. When the crown raised the matter of the indentations in the constable's helmet and how the gun parts found on Day's property linked the weapon to the crime, the judge observed that in his view 'They could have been done by any gun'.

The turning point in the trial undoubtedly came when William entered the witness box. On the night he parted from Day and later spoke to his brothers Henry and Francis. He testified they were both in a very distressed and agitated state. The reason for this was explained by Henry, who told him, 'I have been and killed two policemen,' and added that he believed he had left his cap at the scene.

Henry's barrister insisted his client had made no such confession to his brother. However, Constable Brown, who had accompanied the four prisoners to an early hearing before the local magistrates, told of a conversation he had with Henry, when it was revealed that the cap had been discovered. On the return train journey to the prison, Henry said, 'The cap you've got is mine. I was there and I am a guilty man.' Henry's barrister once again attempted to deny this had been said and suggested the constable was not lying but had misheard his client's words, blaming the notoriously loud third-class railway carriages, in which any conversation was difficult.

The jury was absent for two hours, before finding Day innocent but Francis and Henry were convicted of the constable's murder. However, they recommended mercy as far as Francis was concerned due to his youth and because the killing was not premeditated; no such recommendation was added for Henry. They were sentenced to death and the judge held out little hope of mercy being shown. William was cleared of murdering the constable but the jury did convict him of being an accessory after the fact and recommended he too be shown mercy as he was simply attempting to protect his brothers. The judge rejected this finding as he had not been charged with being an accessory.

The following day, a new jury was sworn in to hear the trial of Day and William, who were charged with the murder of Inspector Drewitt. However, when the prisoners were produced, the prosecutor advised the judge that it had been decided not to proceed with the trial. The reason behind this decision was that he would have to rely on similar evidence to that presented over the previous two days and given they had been cleared, it was felt inappropriate to continue. The judge agreed with this decision and ordered the jury to return a not guilty verdict. This was done and both men were released. However, the prosecutor added that the previous jury's decision regarding William's behaviour had been noted and discussion would take place

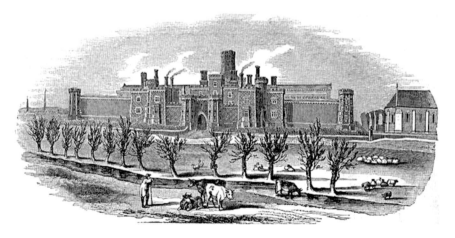

Reading Gaol. (The author)

regarding the possibility of both men being charged with being accessories, but no further charges were ever brought against them.

The convicted men were taken to Reading Gaol and on 24 February, they met with the Visiting Magistrates, to whom both made written confessions. They had shot two pheasants and a jay and were making their way home when they met the two officers, who had apparently heard the gun shots and decided to investigate further. The brothers tried to run away, but Francis was caught and although Henry could have escaped, he returned to rescue his brother.

William Marwood, the hangman. (The author)

The inspector had hold of Francis and as they struggled, Henry shot him and he fell to the ground. Having witnessed this, the constable attempted to flee and Francis shot at him but missed. However, the brothers soon caught up with him and beat him about the head. They returned to Drewitt who was still alive and begged for his life, but he too was beaten to death. The brothers asked that the officers' widows be told they realised how much pain they had caused them and of their genuine remorse.

On 12 March, they were hanged together by William Marwood; it was Henry's twenty-seventh birthday.

14

Constable John Smith
East & West India Docks Police
1877

Ports have played a vital role in the history of the United Kingdom for many centuries and crime has featured greatly throughout their existence. Theft, both petty and major, fraud, smuggling and sabotage, among many other offences, have meant that policing in some form has always been necessary. Prior to the creation of the Port of London Authority Police in the early years of the twentieth century, which later became the Port of Tilbury London Police, several organisations were responsible for policing the capital's docks. One of these was the East and West India Docks Police, which lost just one officer when on duty and that was on the evening of Saturday 26 May 1877.

It was almost five thirty and Constable John Smith and day watchman Thomas Ludlow were at the main entrance to the docks, which was situated on Commercial Road, Poplar. As 27-year-old Robert Brown, a casual labourer, left, the constable suspected he was concealing something under his coat, so approached him and asked what he was attempting to hide. Brown replied, 'Nothing,' and continued walking past him, but Smith was not satisfied and grabbed him by the arm.

Just then a cart was leaving and Ludlow walked towards it in order to check on its contents. As he was doing so, he saw Brown punch Smith in the face as a result of which he staggered backwards. Regaining his composure, he held on to Brown, telling him, 'Now, you must come with me.' However, Brown resisted and as the two men fought, they fell to the ground. A few moments later, Ludlow noticed blood pouring from his colleague's mouth and rushed to assist him.

The East and West India Docks. (The author)

Just then, Inspector Charles Douglas was passing and carried the semi-conscious constable to the police office, from where a doctor was called.

A large crowd witnessed the incident and had helped Ludlow detain Brown, who was told by the inspector that he must accompany him to the office. Brown, however, remained in an uncooperative mood and in a menacing tone of voice told the inspector, 'If you lay a hand on me I will smash your skull in and serve you as I have served that fellow lying in there.' However, he soon realised he had no option other than to comply and eventually agreed to go to the office.

When the inspector advised his prisoner that as he was in such an aggressive frame of mind he considered it necessary to place him in handcuffs, Brown became angrier. Moving his hand behind his back, he pulled out a large billhook, used by dock workers for catching hold of items such as bales of wool, but which could also be a dangerous weapon. Fortunately, the inspector was able to produce his truncheon and strike Brown's arm with such force that he dropped the billhook before any injuries could be caused to him or his men.

It was now that news reached the office confirming that the constable, who had served with the force for six years and was married with four children, was dead. Brown was therefore taken to Poplar police station, where he was charged with the officer's murder. He was held there until Monday morning, when he appeared at the Thames Police Court, where the magistrate, Mr De Rutzen, heard from surgeon Robert Nightingale, who lived in Commercial Road and it was he who had been called to treat Smith, who was dead by the time he arrived. There were no signs of violence and although he had not yet performed a post-mortem he had no hesitation in giving internal haemorrhaging from the lungs as the cause of death. Brown was remanded in custody for one week to await the findings of the post-mortem and the outcome of the inquest, which was to be held within the next few days.

The hearing before Mr De Rutzen resumed on the following Monday and the crown prosecutor revealed that the inquest had taken place and having heard the results of the post-mortem performed by Dr Nightingale, the coroner's jury had decided the constable died of natural causes, clearing Brown of any responsibility for his death. Nevertheless, the crown was determined that he should face trial and as the victim was an on-duty police officer, the appropriate charge was wilful murder. Not surprisingly, Brown's solicitor challenged this by stating that given the decision reached at the inquest, in his opinion, no jury would convict his client of any offence. Given these circumstances, he argued that all charges should be dropped and his client released forthwith.

Dr Nightingale explained to the bench the conclusion he had reached following the post-mortem. He had, as he anticipated, found both lungs in a diseased condition and the left one was in a particularly weakened state as there was a cavity in it. Both lungs had failed and this had caused the fatal haemorrhage. He continued by saying that a punch or kick, even if not inflicted with great force, could have possibly accelerated death, but he had found no signs of violence to the corpse. Mr De Rutzen acknowledged that Smith had been on duty and this would usually lead to a committal on a charge of wilful murder, but he believed there were mitigating circumstances in this case, which meant the charge could be reduced to manslaughter. He respected the decision of the inquest but did not feel bound by it and he therefore committed Brown to stand trial on this lesser charge and granted him bail.

The trial was heard at the Old Bailey on 25 June, at which Brown pleaded not guilty. The crown presented similar evidence to that given at the previous hearings. Under cross examination, Dr Nightingale testified that in his opinion, if the struggle the crown witnesses claimed the defendant had with the deceased did take place, this may possibly have brought the officer's death forward. However, given his poor state of health this would have been by no more than one month.

In his defence, Brown claimed he left the docks in the company of an engine driver, whose name he did not know and it was this man Smith stopped initially in order to search. He continued by saying that it was as he was walking away that the constable attempted to stop him and in so doing, cut the defendant's lip. This had annoyed Brown, who attempted to push the constable's hand away and in the struggle that followed, they fell to the ground. He denied striking Smith in any way and concluded by reminding the court that when searched, no contraband goods were found on him.

The jury found him guilty of manslaughter and he was sentenced to eighteen months imprisonment.

15

Constable George Cole
Metropolitan Police
1882

It had been foggy most of the day, but as night fell on 1 December 1882, it began to clear and at ten fifteen, Eliza Shepherd opened the door of her house, 3, Ashwin Street, Dalston in London, intending to visit a friend. However, just as she was about to step outside, she saw a policeman and another man fighting a few yards away. At first, she thought the officer was attempting to restrain a drunk, but it quickly became clear that it was something far more serious as she saw the man fire a pistol four times at the officer, who staggered backwards, crying out, 'Help me,' as he fell to the ground.

Elizabeth Bucknell lived on nearby Beech Street and was returning home after buying some beer for her father. She also saw the men struggling and ran to alert two policemen she had seen a few minutes

The German Hospital at Dalston, where the injured officer was taken for treatment. (The author)

earlier. Constables James Harford and Patrick Hunt, who rushed to their colleague's assistance, had heard the shots but believed them to have been fog signals. The offender was nowhere to be seen and they found Constable George Cole, lying in the gutter and although very badly injured, he was breathing.

He was taken to the German Hospital, where he was placed in the care of Dr Adolphe Kraus. Unfortunately, he died within minutes of his arrival without having made a statement. Only one of the bullets hit him and this entered his head behind the left ear, shattering his brain, which Dr Kraus would later confirm formally at an inquest, was the cause of death.

The deceased, who was also a member of the Army Reserve Corps, served in N Division of the Metropolitan Police, having joined two years earlier. At the time of his death, he was 27 years old and was living with his wife, Elizabeth, in Lentale Road in Dalston. A few days after the shooting, the following poem appeared in the *Hackney & Kingsland Gazette*:

> Honour his memory, cherish his name!
> He faced the pistol's shot, fought till he fell,
> Fell as a martyr at Duty's cold shrine.
> Facing unequal odds, knowing full well
> Life was the stake at risk. Duty to do,
> Never a thought of self, perhaps one of wife,
> Bravely he faces the certainty Death,
> Copes with determined foe in mortal strife.
>
> Short was the struggle, fatal effect,
> As bravely as fought, as nobly he dies
> Not for the glory of war's martial pomp,
> A martyr to Duty his honoured corpse lies.
> Freely his life he gave for Duty's cause
> Leaving a loving wife mourning his death.
> Picture her sad despair. Helpless and lone,
> God grant she ne'r feels want's chilly breath!
>
> Stretch forth a helping hand, lighten her load,
> That charity further aids Pity's weak hand.

He risked his life and lost, ne'er be it said
His widow shall want in this plenteous land.
Noble his sacrifice willingly given,
Truly a hero, honour his name!
Raise the tall monument telling his deed,
Grave deep the letters that speak of his fame!

Eliza Shepherd and Elizabeth Bucknell's father Robert, who had seen the suspect running from Ashwin Street, gave the police a description of the man. He was said to be aged in his early twenties, be of fair complexion, had a moustache and was about five feet three inches in height. He was wearing light coloured trousers, a long dark overcoat and a black hat, although he was not wearing the hat when he passed Robert. This description was published together with the news that the Home Secretary was offering a reward of £200 to anyone providing information leading to the arrest of the murderer.

Three of the bullets fired by the gunman missed his victim, one having lodged in his truncheon and the other two had hit the walls of nearby houses. The murder weapon was not found, but the police discovered several items of interest. These included a 'wide-awake' hat similar to the one the killer was said to have been wearing and chisels, which it was presumed, the killer would have used as housebreaking tools, were near the entrance of the Baptist Chapel at the corner of Ashwin Street and Beech Street. On one of the chisels, 'rock' had been scratched. It was thought that the constable had believed his killer was intending to break into the chapel and had confronted the suspect, who resisted and drew his weapon with the intention of killing the officer, rather than be taken into custody.

Despite the large reward, little progress was made and there was no arrest. However, this changed in August 1883, when 21-year-old cabinet maker Thomas Orrock appeared in court charged with entering 18, Chard Street, Hoxton, from where he stole two silver watches and other items of jewellery with a combined value of £20, together with gold worth £45.

The owner of the property, Edward Carmichael, told police the accused and his wife lodged with him for seven months until they left

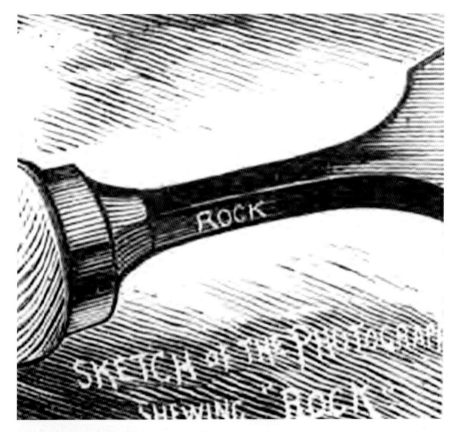

The incriminating chisel, used as evidence to convict the killer. (The Illustrated Police News)

a few days before the burglary. On leaving, Orrock returned two keys, supposedly to the front door of the house, which he had been given when he first rented the rooms. However, it had since been discovered one of the keys was not one of the original pair. That was kept by Orrock, who subsequently used it to gain entry to the premises. However, as he was leaving, he was recognised by a neighbour, which led to his arrest. He was found guilty of the crime and taken to Clerkenwell Gaol to begin his sentence of twelve months imprisonment. The police had by then begun to take an interest in Orrock as they believed he fitted the description of the Dalston murderer. Furthermore, it was learnt that he knew the chapel on Ashwin Street very well as he and his parents worshipped there regularly and he and his wife were married there

Arthur Evans. (The Illustrated Police News)

Frederick Miles. (The Illustrated Police News)

shortly after the constable's murder. The investigation now focused on Orrock and his associates, who realising the possible serious consequences for themselves if they did not cooperate, provided the police with a great deal of helpful information.

Two young men in particular helped the police to build a case against Orrock and they were Arthur Evans and Frederick Miles, who had spent much of the day and evening of the murder in the suspect's company and they were able to confirm that he was wearing clothes similar to those described by the witnesses who had seen the killer running away. Evans and Miles had spent several hours on the day in question drinking in pubs in and around Dalston and at eight o'clock were in the Railway Tavern. This was near the chapel on Ashwin Street, which Orrock now told them he planned to break into and steal a quantity of plate he knew to be in the building and which he intended to have melted down. He showed them a number of chisels he would use to force entry into the building if necessary and a revolver, telling his friends, 'I will have no hesitation in using this if anyone should interfere with me.'

A service was being held in the chapel and Orrock left, saying he hoped to enter unseen and unfasten the latch of a window, through which he would later be able to gain entry, without having to use the chisels. He returned after an absence of a few minutes, content that he had been able to complete his task, but said it was much darker than he had anticipated and Evans accompanied him to a nearby shop where he bought a lamp for eightpence. They returned to the pub, where they remained until ten o'clock, when Orrock stood and told his friends that he was going to break into the chapel. Evans and Miles remained in the pub until they heard what at first they believed to be a series of fog signals. However, they went outside to investigate with a group of other drinkers to see the constable lying in the gutter, at which point the two men separated and left the area.

A few days later, Orrock approached them both, concerned that they might be tempted to report what they knew in view of the reward now being offered. However, they assured him they would not do so and swore an oath to reinforce this pledge. He told Evans later that Cole approached him, suspecting correctly that he was about to break into the chapel and when he attempted to run off, the constable grabbed hold of him to prevent him from doing so. Orrock insisted that he threw the revolver several feet away as they struggled as he realized he would receive more than three months imprisonment for attempted burglary, if found in possession of the weapon. However, Cole managed to take hold of it and as they continued to struggle, Orrock had panicked and pulled the trigger.

Another young man who provided important information was Henry Mortimer, who was serving a one year prison sentence for burglary when police interviewed him. He confirmed he had been with Orrock after he had bought the revolver some weeks before the crime and went with him to Tottenham Marshes, where he practised using it by firing into a tree. This tree was identified and a bullet retrieved, which was similar to those found at the murder scene. Mortimer also told police that Orrock purchased the weapon and twenty-five cartridges for ten shillings after seeing it advertised in *Exchange and Mart* in early October, from Jose MacLellan. He and his wife were taken to see Orrock but were unable to positively identify him as the purchaser. The revolver

Henry Mortimer. (The Illustrated Police News)

was never found and another friend, Richard Green, reported that he was told by Orrock that he had thrown it into an unidentified stretch of water.

William Ames, another acquaintance, had often taken the chisels used by Orrock at work to be ground at Preston's Tool Shop in Shoreditch. The proprietor, Ann Preston, said she often scratched the names of the owner of the tools on them to make them easily recognisable. However, when shown the one with 'rock' on it, which was discovered at the crime scene she could not say definitely that she was responsible for making the mark, explaining 'I am not much of a scholar for writing'. It was examined under a strong microscope by chemist James Cameron, who was convinced he could discern the letters 'o' and 'r' in front of 'rock', implying it did indeed belong to the suspected murderer.

Some of those who provided the incriminating information, which formed the basis of the crown's case against Orrock, could have faced charges, but none did so and testified for the prosecution at the trial which opened at the Old Bailey on 19 September 1884. Admittedly, the crown's case was largely circumstantial, but it proved to be sufficient to convict him and led to him being sentenced to death.

He was taken to the condemned cell in Newgate and he accepted that the nature of the crime meant there was no prospect of a reprieve. He was visited regularly by his wife, mother and step-father and also by Reverend W.H. Burton, the minister of the Baptist Chapel on Ashwin Street, which he had intended to burgle. As his execution drew closer, he made a full confession but added the act was not premeditated. He was hanged on the morning of October 6 by James Berry alongside Thomas Harris who was convicted of the murder of his wife at Kilburn.

16

Constable Alexander Lamond
Kirkcaldy Burgh Police
1883

The Kirkcaldy Burgh Police had received many complaints over a period of several weeks from residents living in the harbour area, regarding a house on High Street, which was situated between the bonded warehouses and the Harbour Head Hotel. The house was rented by Jane Murdoch, who with two other women, Catherine Marr and Rachel Thomas, who was also known as 'Notorious Rachel', had opened what was essentially a drinking den and brothel. Following yet another report of a rowdy disturbance at eleven o'clock on the night of 25 May 1883, Constables Alexander Lamond and Robert Mays were ordered to make their way to the premises and restore order.

The officers discovered that four men were being entertained by the women and all had been drinking heavily. The men were licenced hawkers, visiting the town from Dundee and they were John Doig, 33-year-old Charles McGinnis, together with brothers James and Alexander Young, 30 and 27 respectively. On their arrival, the officers were subjected to a great deal of verbal abuse and after ten minutes the men and women had not been persuaded to quieten down and Lamond suggested his colleague should leave and return with more officers. Several arrived to find the front door open and three of the hawkers to have left.

Lamond had by this time staggered out into the street in a state of collapse and he was taken to the Harbour Head Hotel, where he was treated by Drs Alexander Curror and Henry Gordon. He had suffered extensive cuts and bruises to the whole of his body, but most damage was done to his head and face, which included badly swollen

Kirkcaldy Harbour in the late nineteenth century. (The author)

eyelids and wounds to his forehead, left ear and nose. There were seven major scalp wounds, which had exposed the skull. He died at six o'clock in the morning, without having regained consciousness. A post mortem was performed at the hotel by the two doctors, which revealed massive internal injuries and his skull was fractured in two places, leading them to conclude that death was caused by a cerebral haemorrhage.

The three women had remained in the house together with Doig, all of whom surrendered to the police on their arrival and all co-operated, meaning a clear picture emerged immediately of what occurred after Mays had left the property. It was accepted that Doig had attempted to prevent the other men from assaulting their victim and that he himself had been injured as he was doing so.

After his colleague had left, Lamond locked the front door to prevent anyone from leaving and placed the key in his pocket. His attackers seized his truncheon with which they began their attack and after he fell to the floor, they used a chair and the fender which they took from the fireplace, with which to continue beating him. In a desperate attempt to escape the blows, Lamond unlocked the door, enabling the attackers to flee. Then, they took a boat from its moorings in the harbour, but its rowlocks were missing and failing to make any headway, they headed for the shore. They returned to their lodgings in Hill Place, but in view of the information given by Doig, the police were waiting for them and the three men were arrested without difficulty.

The constable's body was taken to his lodgings on Nicol Street, from where, on the following Tuesday, the hearse carrying his body, set off for Kirkcaldy Cemetery. It was accompanied by a large number of officers from the local and surrounding forces, local officials and his two brothers led the family mourners. Unfortunately, all did not go according to plan as the family had asked that the funeral take place earlier than originally planned and a telegram advising six members of the Edinburgh City Police of these new arrangements was delayed and not received by them, which led to those officers arriving late.

Within days of the killing, the *Fife Free Press* carried a letter from the dead constable's brother:

> 'Sir, I, the undersigned do hereby beg through your columns, respectfully to thank the Provost, magistrates and Police Commissioners of the burgh of Kirkcaldy, for the extreme amount of kindness and courtesy shown to me and to my friends in connection with the unfortunate death of my brother, Alexander Lamond, late police constable in the Kirkcaldy Burgh Police Force; and for the kindness and courtesy I further beg to thank Mr Chalmers, the Superintendent of Police and those under him. JOHN H LAMOND 29th May, 1883.'

The *Fifeshire Advertiser* included a letter from a local resident, concerned at the circumstances leading to the constable's death, which reflected the views of many who lived in the town:

> 'Sir, As it has been for some time back known to the police that the house in which last Friday evening's tragic event took place was a house frequented by persons, both male and female, of the most questionable character, I would like to be informed if there is no local act or burgh bye-law in existence empowering the magistrates to stamp out such dens in our midst? Anyone conniving at the purpose for which such a house is upheld is an enemy to all public morality, charity and order. In short,

he is playing into the hands of the devil himself and takes upon his shoulders a grave responsibility, which few, be he Jew or Gentile, would be inclined to incur. I am &c, COPPERFIELD. 1st June 1883.'

The first court case to be heard arising from the events which ended with the constable's death was that involving Rachel Thompson, who was accused of creating a breach of the peace that night. She had made many such appearances in the police court, hence her nickname 'Notorious Rachel', but this was the first occasion on which anyone could recall her looking so terrified. On entering the dock, she immediately lay down but stood when ordered to do so. However, she refused to face the bench and stood with her back towards the magistrates throughout the hearing. She pleaded guilty and when told she was to be sentenced to a term of imprisonment for sixty days without the option of paying a fine, she let out a piercing scream and was led down into the cells crying uncontrollably.

The three men accused of murder appeared in the lower court to be committed for trial and there appeared to be little doubt that the case against them was extremely strong, especially as there were witnesses to the crime. Alexander Young obviously realised the significance of their evidence and was heard to make a threat against Doig from the dock as the witness walked past him. Their trial was scheduled to open later that summer and forty-eight witnesses were listed to appear. However, they were not required as the Advocate-Depute advised the Court he was prepared to accept the men's guilty pleas to the lesser charge of culpable homicide.

He explained that there was an absence of premeditation and the accused believed the officer had no right to lock the door and prevent them from leaving the house. Indeed, it was accepted that Lamond had told them he only intended charging the women with keeping a disorderly house, but when they attempted to leave, he had prevented them from doing so by locking the door. The hawkers acknowledged struggling with him but the intention was not to kill or cause injury, but simply to leave the property. Another factor confirming the crime was not planned was the fact that only weapons immediately to hand at the scene, including the officer's baton, were used. They had drunk to excess and although this was no excuse for what they did, it had led them to behave uncharacteristically as all were said to be of previous good character.

The judge agreed that culpable homicide was the appropriate charge but emphasised it was still a very serious matter as three of them had attacked one man. He continued by saying, 'It is therefore necessary, as a warning to others, that the sentence must be commensurate with the gravity of the offence' and he sentenced each of them to ten years penal servitude.

17

Constable Alfred Austwick
West Riding of Yorkshire Constabulary
1886

Constable Alfred Austwick of the West Riding Constabulary was walking towards his home at 3, Church Hill, Dodworth, when he met miner Gheo Thickett. It was eleven o'clock at night on Saturday 31 July 1886 and the two men chatted as they approached the Traveller's Inn, where they stopped, on the corner of Lambert Fold, close to where the constable lived. Several men had gathered there after a night's drinking and among them were miners Joseph Lodge and John Brown together with Fred Lodge, an underground engine driver at the Strafford Main Colliery. Also there was James Murphy, who was standing in the middle of the road, shouting so loudly that he was causing great annoyance to those living nearby. The constable knew Murphy lived on Lambert Fold and suggested he should go home. Sadly, Murphy did not heed this good advice and what happened next was witnessed by several of the men at the scene, who were able to provide a graphic account of what followed.

All were agreed that Murphy had been drinking but was not drunk and as far as they were concerned, he knew exactly what he was doing. When he saw the constable, who stood well over six feet in height, Murphy, who was five feet four inches tall, approached him and said menacingly, 'It is you. Stop here until I come back,' before stepping into the darkness of Lambert Fold.

Joseph Lodge informed the constable that a few minutes before he appeared, he heard Murphy shout, 'That's where he lives, him I want,' as he pointed towards the officer's house. This led the men to suggest they feared Murphy was intent on causing mischief of some kind and urged Austwick to leave. However, he was still on duty and was not prepared to be intimidated and replied, 'No, I am not frightened.' Murphy returned moments later holding a gun, which he raised, saying as he did so, 'Where are we now?' He fired without warning at the constable, who fell to the ground, as his assailant screamed at him, 'You are paid for it,' before running off.

David McCoubrey, a surgeon, who lived in the village, was asked to attend the scene and he found the constable lying on the ground, barely conscious. He noticed a hole on the left side of his tunic, which was saturated with blood. Having heard the shot, several neighbours arrived and helped carry the constable, who remained conscious, to his home. Interestingly, as his uniform was being removed, it was discovered that his watch had been shattered by the bullet and had stopped at the exact moment he was hit. His wound was bound with cold water bandages and he was given morphia to ease the pain. Nevertheless, his pulse remained weak and intermittent and he died at twenty minutes to one.

Mr McCoubrey performed a post-mortem on the Monday morning and gave the results at the inquest, which was held later that afternoon

DETERMINED MURDER of A POLICEMAN near BARNSLEY

Constable Austwick is shot in cold blood. (The Illustrated Police News)

in the Traveller's Inn. He had removed the scalp and found there were no injuries to the head or brain. There was a wound located six inches below the left nipple, from which part of the stomach and mesentery protruded. There were massive internal injuries; the heart was displaced; there was severe damage to the left lung, the spleen, left kidney and the liver; and several ribs had been fractured. The cause of death was heart failure from shock and loss of blood, the result of the single gunshot wound.

One of those who carried the dying man home was local schoolmaster, Mr R.N. Penlington. He advised the coroner that when it was realised the constable might die before a death bed deposition could be taken by a law officer, he asked him if he knew who had shot him and received the reply, 'Murphy. I was standing in front of Buckle's butcher's shop when Murphy came out and shot me.'

Afterwards, the witnesses at the scene of the shooting, faced criticism for not attempting to grab the gun to prevent Murphy pulling the trigger and for failing to follow the killer after the shooting. However, it was later accepted that Murphy had acted so quickly, without giving any warning, which meant they had not been aware of the weapon in his hand before it was fired, nor had they attempted to pursue Murphy as they, like most of the residents of Dodworth, were terrified of him when he was in a belligerent mood.

The deceased was born and raised in Lumby in South Milford, where his father was employed as a farm bailiff. As a boy, Austwick attended the local Wesleyan School and upon leaving, found work with the North Eastern Railway Company. He left to join the West Riding Constabulary as a 19-year-old, serving at Wakefield, Barnsley, Gawber and Worsbrough. However, in his early twenties, he became disillusioned, which led to his resigning and rejoining the railway company as a signalman at Goole. It was here that he met his wife Sarah and they were to have seven children, two of whom died when young.

In October 1881, he re-joined the West Riding Constabulary and two months later was posted to Dodworth, where he and his family set up home. The young family became popular with their neighbours, who came to view their village constable as good natured and fair minded. His murder came as a great shock and in its immediate aftermath Sarah received much support from her neighbours, many of whom were there to bid him farewell, as it had been decided he would be buried in South Milford, where his grieving parents still lived.

In view of his large size, Mr F.W. Ownsworth, Dodworth's undertaker, had to make a huge pine coffin especially, bearing a brass plate, which read 'Alfred Austwick, died August 1st 1886 aged 32 years'. As it was leaving the house, the Dodworth Church Choir sang a number of suitable hymns and it was soon covered with many wreaths thrown by villagers and police colleagues lining the route to Dodworth Station.

As the train carrying the coffin entered South Milford Station, the platform and bridge which crossed the line, were packed with hundreds of people, who were there to pay their respects to a man many of them had known well. The coffin was placed in a cart provided by George Webster, the farmer for whom the deceased's father had worked since 1854. His relatives and other mourners were taken to the churchyard in ten carts, loaned by the village's farmers and tradesmen. As the procession passed through the village, women were seen to weep and the men to remove their hats and bow their heads. The coffin was carried to the graveside by six Barnsley police officers and he was interred alongside his brother who had been crushed to death in an accident, five years earlier.

When it was learnt that Sarah would be entitled to one payment of £25 only, from the West Riding Police Superintendent Fund, a group of Dodworth residents decide to start a subscription fund on her behalf. The objective was to raise enough with which to purchase an annuity, which would provide her with a weekly payment of ten shillings. One of the earliest donations was one of £25 given by the Barnsley Magistrates, who had known the dead man well.

The 45-year-old fugitive was born in Barnsley, the son of a hand-loom weaver, who moved to Dodworth with his family when Murphy was eight years old. He was one of five children, two of whom died young. His remaining siblings were a sister, Mary Ann and two brothers, Michael, a miner living at Kinsley Common and Patrick, a professional cricketer with Broughton Cricket Club in Salford.

James Murphy. (The author)

Murphy had been a miner all his working life and was viewed as a good workman by his colleagues in the pits. He was married with two children, a daughter who was in domestic service and an 11-year old-son.

As a young man, he began to drink heavily and could become violent. He also turned to poaching on a regular basis and other criminal behaviour including theft and burglary. In all, he made twenty-five appearances before Barnsley Magistrates and the Assize Courts, which had led to many fines. He had also served terms of imprisonment in Wakefield Gaol, one of which in 1877 was a sentence of three months for threatening a police sergeant with a gun whilst poaching. The following year, he was sentenced to five years penal servitude for housebreaking. On another occasion, he threatened to kill two of his managers at the Church Lane Colliery in Dodworth. His last conviction was on 6 May 1885, for poaching.

A motive for the crime had emerged as the search for Murphy began. Earlier on the day of the shooting, Murphy had visited the Station Hotel in Dodworth. He told Henry Burgess, the landlord, that on the previous evening, the constable had served him with a summons to appear before the local Police Court on the following Wednesday. He was to face a charge of being drunk and behaving in a riotous manner, which Austwick had witnessed and reported. Murphy added, 'He has served this on me, but he will never have to serve another because I will blow a hole through him.'

The landlord did not take this threat seriously, having heard Murphy make many similar statements in the past. However, it seems that he had felt aggrieved about Austwick's attitude towards him and his family for some time. He had spoken of the officer stopping him in the street regularly to search him. He also described many occasions on which he was said to have stopped Murphy's children in the street to ask about their father's movements, the names of any visitors and whether they had rabbits or hares at meal times.

The police were aware that it might prove difficult to find Murphy, for as a collier he knew of all the disused pit workings over a wide area, in which he might find shelter. Furthermore, having been a poacher in the district for many years, he would know every hedge, ditch and barn in which to hide. Nevertheless, it was decided to extend the search over a much wider area and friends in Manchester and Stockport were visited. On one occasion, he was said to have been seen dressed as a woman in Woolley, but as the weeks passed without any sightings, it was thought by many that he had probably committed suicide.

The police paid regular and unannounced visits to the homes of his brothers, believing he might have approached them for help. Such visits were also made to the home of William Goss, the brother of Murphy's wife, who lived at Barugh and where he was almost captured on the afternoon of 15 September. Superintendents Kane and Stansfield along with Detective Inspector Ramsden called at the house and a search was made. Murphy was found in one of the bedrooms but was able to escape by jumping out of the window after threatening the inspector with his gun. However, it was now known that he was still alive.

He remained at liberty for another two days only. Detective Sergeant Lodge and several colleagues visited the home of Murphy's friend, John Henderson, a miner living at Kingstone Place. Murphy was in a bedroom and when confronted by the sergeant, he levelled his gun at him, but Lodge was able to push the barrel aside with his umbrella. Murphy pulled the trigger but the bullet missed the sergeant and he was arrested and taken to Barnsley.

William Goss and John Henderson were both put on trial as accessories after the fact, having offered Murphy shelter. They pleaded not guilty, claiming Murphy had visited their houses but he always had his gun with him and they were in fear of him. However, they were convicted and Henderson was sentenced to three weeks imprisonment in York Castle. The jury which found Goss guilty made a strong recommendation for mercy, which led the judge to impose a conditional discharge.

Murphy appeared at the York Winter Assizes on 9 November at which his barrister claimed his client was insane. This was rejected by the jury and he was found guilty of wilful murder and sentenced to death. There was no significant attempt to obtain a reprieve and the condemned man remained unrepentant, saying he had no regrets about killing the constable.

On the eve of his execution, Murphy wrote the following letter to his wife:

'Dear Wife,

I write these few lines hoping you are all well as it leaves me at present. On Monday I shall meet my death and shall know the great secret. There is no mercy for me, so I must die; and I hope you will all together give me a prayer and I will meet my fate as brave as I can. I hope my dear wife, you will think of the next world and our next meeting, for you will not be here for ever. So farewell dear wife and farewell dear children too. Dear brothers and relations for this life we all must part, may the Lord have mercy on you all. JAMES MURPHY.'

Looking back on his career in the book *My Experiences as an Executioner*, published in 1892, James Berry wrote of Murphy's final hours, before his execution at York Castle on 29 November 1886.

He was a Roman Catholic but refused to see a priest. Berry, accompanied by the prison governor, was introduced to him on the eve of the hanging and held a conversation with him. The condemned man asked the governor jokingly, for a pipe of tobacco, which he of course knew he could not have. He then asked Berry to dispatch him as quickly and painlessly as possible, which the hangman confirms he was able to do a few hours later.

In February 1887, the fund opened on behalf of Mrs Austwick and her children, closed after £516.3s.2d had been raised.

James Berry, the hangman.
(The author)

18

Superintendent Thomas Birkill
West Riding of Yorkshire Constabulary
1887

38-year old-William Taylor was the son of a prosperous farmer at Norwood in Yorkshire who had begun to behave strangely in his childhood. When, in later life, he attempted to help his father manage the family farm, he was unable to cope with the responsibility and had to give it up, after which he had no meaningful employment of any kind. His situation was not helped when he began to drink heavily and accumulate convictions for being drunk and riotous. Despite Taylor's often disturbed behaviour and heavy drinking, he held a licence for a double-barrelled shotgun and a number of local farmers allowed him to shoot on their land.

He was eventually disowned by his father, who nevertheless, following his errant son's marriage, paid his rent and gave him a weekly allowance, although his wife Hannah was often required to take cleaning jobs to supplement the family income. In 1887, he, his wife and their two daughters, ten weeks old Annie and Elizabeth who was five years of age, were living on Cambridge Road in Otley. It was an unhappy marriage and Taylor was often violent towards Hannah, who lived in fear of him. Also living with them was their lodger Ellis Brumfitt Hartley, a gardener.

Midnight was approaching on Wednesday 23 November when the Taylors and their lodger went to bed, but Annie, who was ill with bronchitis, could not sleep and was coughing to such an extent that she woke Ellis, who went downstairs and lit a fire. Hannah was also unable to sleep and she too made her way to the living room, taking Annie with her, intending to make a poultice for her. Shortly afterwards, she and Ellis heard her husband getting out of bed,

Otley at the time of the superintendent's murder. (The author)

prompting Hannah to open the front and back doors, should the need arise for her to escape her husband's wrath.

Taylor was indeed in an angry and aggressive mood when he joined them and demanded to know why his sleep had been disturbed and the reason his wife had opened the doors. She assured him that it was to create a draught for the fire. Taylor slammed both doors shut and said he would encourage the fire to burn by firing his gun up the chimney. As he took hold of the firearm, he began to threaten her as she had feared, saying he would swing for her.

As the anxious Ellis ran out of the front door, Hannah still had Annie in her arms and now terrified that her husband would carry out his threat, she made for the back door, which she flung open and ran into the yard. Taylor ran after her, raised the weapon and fired. Her clothing was singed although the bullet missed her and she sought refuge with her neighbours Edwin and Mary Freeman. She had been there for a few minutes when blood was seen dripping from the blanket in which Annie was wrapped and it was realised the baby had been hit by the bullet and badly wounded. Dr William Bennett arrived to treat her wound, but Annie died at four thirty.

The gunshot was heard by Constable John Shippam and he approached the cottage. Taylor had by now locked the doors and when the constable demanded to know what had occurred and to be let in, he shouted, 'I isn't up yet.' Having failed to gain entry and hearing Taylor shout, 'Come on, I's ready for thee,' Shippam left to seek support. A short time later several officers were outside the cottage, including Shippam and Constable Richard Wildman. However, Taylor was not about to surrender to the officers, who could see through the window that he was still holding his shotgun. He underlined the threat he posed by shouting, 'I'll make it warm for anyone who tries to get in.' Taylor's brother Stephen agreed to try and persuade him to surrender but his pleas were ignored and the siege continued.

It was now seven thirty and it was decided to alert Superintendent Thomas Birkill, the senior officer at Otley, who arrived to take control of the situation. He ordered two of his officers to stand at the rear entrance as he, Shippam and Wildman went to the front of the house. Using a crowbar, the superintendent attempted to prise the door open, telling his colleagues, 'I'll keep him engaged here until they get him at the back.' However, rather than try to escape by the back door, Taylor shot through window at the superintendent, who was little more than two feet away from him, causing massive injuries to his head. He fell into Wildman's arms and still breathing, he was carried to a neighbour's house, where he received medical attention, but died later that morning.

As soon as the superintendent had been shot, a telegram was sent to Inspector John Crow, who was stationed at Ilkley and he reached

Taylor shoots his baby daughter. (The Illustrated Police News)

the scene at nine-thirty. He was given details of the gunman and believed he might be enticed out of the cottage, by making him believe the police had left the area. He therefore ordered all his men to remain silent and to hide from Taylor's view. The ploy worked, as some time later, Taylor opened the back door carrying a knife and shovel, as though he was about to fetch some coal from a shed in the yard, but he was grabbed and handcuffed. A search of the premises revealed that his daughter Elizabeth was unharmed in an upstairs bedroom. By this time a large crowd had gathered outside the cottage and a loud cheer went up when it was learnt Taylor was in police custody. He was put in a cab to be taken to Otley Police Station and as it moved off he shouted to the crowd, 'Hello lads, I don't care now I've got my revenge.'

Post-mortems were performed on both bodies within a few hours of the shootings. Dr Bennett found a large wound to Annie's back; her lower spine was shattered and her intestines were protruding. Following her death, Dr Bennett was standing at the Freemans' front door and saw the superintendent outside of Taylor's cottage with the crowbar in his hands. After hearing a gunshot, he watched as the officer staggered backwards before falling to the ground. The wounded man was brought to him, but there was nothing that could be done to save him. He was bleeding heavily from a wound just above his left ear, which had resulted in a fractured skull and he died without regaining consciousness. Thus, Dr Bennett had the unusual distinction of performing a post-mortem on the victim of a murder he himself had witnessed.

When Taylor was charged with the double murder by Inspector Crow, also present was the police surgeon Dr Pinder, who had examined the prisoner following his arrest. The doctor had mentioned the shooting of Annie, but Taylor insisted he was not responsible. When charged he said, 'I think I have done it a bit too far this time, with drink.' Later that night, Taylor was visited by surgeon Mr Ritchie, who had treated him for the past twenty years and during their conversation a reason for the shooting emerged as Taylor said he suspected his wife of putting poison in the medicine she was giving to their daughter and he was attempting to shoot her to prevent her from poisoning the little girl.

A joint inquest was held into the deaths of Annie and the superintendent, which was followed by a committal hearing before the town's magistrates. At both hearings, questions were raised concerning the prisoner's state of mind but it was made clear by the coroner and chairman of the bench that any ruling as to whether he was sane or not, would have to be decided at the higher court.

Superintendent Birkill, who left a widow and an adult son, joined the West Riding Police thirty years earlier and during his career served at Doncaster, Wakefield and Normanton, where he was serving as an inspector, when promoted to superintendent and transferred to Otley in 1878. That he was respected by colleagues and others became evident at the inquest and in the magistrates' court.

At the close of the inquest, after Taylor was taken from the chamber, Mr W.L. Williams, who represented the police, rose to his feet and expressed his deep regret at the officer's death. He had known him for many years and described him as a most able officer. This was echoed by Taylor's solicitor, John Gledstone, who had known the deceased for ten years. The coroner agreed with these sentiments and believed him to have been a most able man, who always performed his duty in the best possible way. A member of the jury, who had also known him, called out, 'Not only his efficiency but his kindness also.'

Following Taylor's committal for trial, the chairman of the magistrates, Mr Ayscough Fawkes observed:

> 'On many occasions, when sitting in this chair, I had constantly to refer to the superintendent in cases which came before the court and instead of being harsh, he always tended to leniency and if anyone had trouble he was always willing to assist them and do his best'.

Taylor's trial was held at the West Riding Winter Assizes sitting at Leeds Town Hall on 16 February 1888, with a request made by his barrister that a decision should be made as to whether his client was fit to plead. A jury was sworn in to consider this and the judge emphasised that they were not to determine if he was sane or otherwise, but simply if he was aware at the present time of the difference between pleading guilty and not guilty.

Doctor Clifford Allbutt, who had interviewed the prisoner on two occasions at the request of the defence, was called to the stand. He stated that in his opinion Taylor was an epileptic and seemed to be weak-minded, incoherent and confused. He had told the witness that he was born with what he described as four endowments, namely health, strength, prosperity and knowledge, which were bestowed on him by one of the two gods he believed existed. When the murders were raised with him, he denied killing Annie but had some slight memory of the superintendent's death.

The doctor acknowledged he was possibly feigning this confused state of mind but thought it unlikely. To conclude his evidence, he said that the accused was not capable of giving proper instructions to his barrister or to fully appreciate the seriousness of his present situation. This finding was supported by Dr Wright, consultant physician to the Wakefield Lunatic Asylum. Further supporting evidence was given not by medical professionals but by those who had known him in the recent and more distant past. Both his solicitor, Mr Gledstone and Reverend Thomas Brooks, who had known him and his family for twenty years, believed him to be delusional.

Since his arrest, Taylor had spent time in the gaols at Wakefield and in Armley at Leeds and the crown called the medical staff from both institutions. All agreed that he had eaten and slept well and enjoyed good physical health during this period of remand. When engaged in conversation, he appeared to possess a clear understanding of any question put to him and answered coherently. According to these witnesses, no symptoms of insanity had been exhibited.

The jury found that he was fit to plead and the trial proper was opened with a new jury. The crown continued to insist that the defendant was putting on a convincing act but was sane. It was argued that Taylor knew what he was doing, as he used a loaded gun to resist arrest, because he knew he had done wrong in shooting the superintendent. They posed the question that if he was experiencing uncontrollable homicidal tendencies, why did he not attack his daughter Elizabeth who was in the cottage?

The defence persisted with its claim that Taylor was not of sound mind and called his mother Elizabeth, who described her son as being a normal happy child until he was six years old, when he contracted scarlet fever and began suffering epileptic fits, which would continue throughout his life. He had acted strangely ever since and his condition became even worse when he was severely beaten by a gang of men at a local fair when he was twenty years of age. He had been unable to work and would not have survived without the financial and emotional support of his family. Taylor's brother Stephen and two former workmates gave similar testimony.

Dr Wright said that in his opinion, if a request had been made, on the day of the murders, to admit Taylor to a lunatic asylum, such a request would most certainly have been agreed to. Having heard this evidence, the judge advised the jury that if they believed the defendant was of unsound mind, they should make this clear when delivering their verdict. They retired for twenty-five minutes before convicting him of both murders but adding he was of unsound mind at the time. The judge ordered that he be detained during Her Majesty's pleasure.

19

Sergeant Enos Molden
Wiltshire Constabulary
1892

29-year-old John Gurd was one of three brothers and in late 1890 was living with his widowed mother in Shaftesbury when, using the name Louis Hamilton, he applied successfully for the position of attendant at the Wiltshire Lunatic Asylum in Devizes. It was here that he met 21-year-old housemaid Florence Adams and after a brief courtship they became engaged. A date was set for the wedding and

The Wiltshire Lunatic Asylum, where Gurd met and fell in love with Florence Adams. (The author)

the banns were read for the first time on 3 April 1892. It was decided by the couple that he should quit his job and seek more remunerative employment and he left two days later on the fifth.

However, Miss Spencer, the institution's housekeeper, now advised Florence that her fiancé owed a great deal of money and had even borrowed from patients in the asylum, none of which had been repaid, Florence became extremely upset on hearing this and wrote to him, breaking off the engagement because of what she had discovered and telling him that she never wanted to see him again. On Saturday, 9 April, she received this reply:

'Shaftesbury, Dorset.

My Dear Flo, Please forgive me for taking the liberty of writing to you again, but do please read this before you throw it into the fire. O, my dear, I am broken hearted and I have sent this to ask your forgiveness. My dear, I know I am guilty, but it is through you Flo my dear, that I was in such difficulties. You know Flo my dear, or at least you must think that it has cost me a lot of money to do as I have when I have been out with you. Now, dear Flo, that I am ruined you look on me with scorn. But never mind. When I can I will return to Devizes and pay every penny and follow you until the end of the world. I will have a bitter revenge some day; if not on you, I will on your old people or someone. Take notice of this for I mean it; that is if you give me up. But O darling, do please forgive me for the wrong I have done you and don't get married just yet; give me time, Flo dear, to get over this and pay what I owe. I will pay every penny when I can; indeed I will and have you too my dear, if you will have mercy on me. Do ask Harry (Richards) and dad (Florence's grandfather) to think of me as well as they can, for if any poor wretch was in need of their pity, I am now. O dear Flo, look at it, I have done no crime; I only owe some money, which I will pay as soon as I can. I am going to America. Now dear, don't tell where I am, my dear, I mean not to the police, for the sake of better times. I know you will not, my dear. I will take care of the ring until we meet again and I know we shall some day and then if you are a wife you shall die.

L. HAMILTON. P.S. O my dear Flo, have mercy on me; don't get married.'

Gurd wasted no time in taking his revenge on Florence and later that Saturday night, he travelled to Melksham, where Henry Richards, her uncle, lived. He was one of the men named in his letter and Gurd found him in the King's Arms, where he joined him for a glass of beer. Henry was unaware his niece had ended the engagement and had no reason to fear Gurd, who showed no signs of hostility. The other drinkers later said they left apparently on friendly terms and made their way to the Crown public house, where again they drank together.

On leaving the Crown, the two men walked a short distance along the path of the nearby canal, when without warning, Gurd took a revolver from his pocket and shot Henry twice in the back. Several people were in the vicinity and initially believed children were playing with fireworks but came to realise they were gunshots when Henry was heard to shout, 'I'm a dead man!' He had been shot twice in the back and could not be saved. One of those close to the shooting knew Gurd and told the police he had seen him running away, so the search for him began immediately.

The police search extended over a wide area, but Gurd was able to avoid capture for a few days, visiting Bath and Frome. At ten-thirty on the Monday night, he was in Corsley, where he called at the White Hart Inn. However, the landlord had died a few days before and was buried earlier that day. His widow and two of his brothers were having a quiet drink inside and ignored Gurd, who was knocking on the locked door, but he realised there were people drinking inside and took exception to not being admitted. Moments later, the mourners were startled by a gunshot and on investigating, discovered that a horse tethered at the door had been shot and badly injured. The owner of the injured horse took it immediately for treatment by a vet in Warminster and called at the police station to report the matter.

Superintendent Perrett, suspected that Gurd was possibly responsible and although it was now three o'clock in the morning, decided to make for Corsley and set off with Constables Davies and Langley, together with Sergeant Enos Molden. A little later, as the four officers approached Longleat Park, they saw a man walking towards them. It was Gurd and as he drew level with them he noticed their uniforms, prompting him to ask the superintendent, 'Do you want me Sir? Here I am.' The superintendent replied, 'I think I do, for the murder of the man at Melksham.' However, rather than surrender, Gurd stepped back and took his revolver from a pocket. The officers pounced on him, but he was able to fire twice in rapid succession. The first missed but the second hit the sergeant to the left side of his body. He shouted to Constable Davies, 'Oh dear Davies, I am shot. Take hold of me, I am dying,' before collapsing into his colleague's arms

The superintendent and Langley overpowered Gurd, who was disarmed and handcuffed without another shot being fired. The sergeant, who was still breathing, was carried to the nearby Whitbourn Cottage, where he died fifteen minutes later, before a doctor could reach him. Gurd had also been taken to the cottage and was in the room when the sergeant died. The prisoner was escorted to the police station at Warminster and the sergeant's body was taken to his home. The weapon used in both murders was a six-chambered revolver and the prisoner was carrying a large number of bullets in his pockets.

Sergeant Molden, who was 49 years old, left a widow and four children. He had served in the Wiltshire force for almost thirty years, eleven of them as a sergeant. He was transferred to Warminster just three months before his death and before that he was stationed in Shrewton for ten years. He was due to return to the village the day after he was shot, to receive a farewell gift of a purse of £12 and a marble clock, which the villagers were intending to present him with, to mark the respect in which they held him.

Following his arrest, Gurd made no attempt to deny responsibility for the two shootings. He acknowledged that he travelled to Melksham with the sole intent of killing Henry Richards, as he blamed him for being largely responsible for turning his niece against him and urging her to break off the engagement, a claim later refuted by Florence. Gurd added that if he had met Florence in the days he was at large, he would have shot her also. He regretted shooting the sergeant, which he said was done in the heat of the moment as he was attempting to escape.

Surgeon Mr R. L. Willcox made a preliminary examination of the sergeant's body and confirmed one bullet had entered five inches below the left nipple. An internal examination revealed that the bullet was lodged close to the right kidney, after hitting the eighth rib, then turning downwards and passing through the spleen and then lacerating the abdominal aorta, this causing an internal haemorrhage.

Gurd was charged with both murders and in the days that followed, joint inquests and committal proceedings before the town's magistrates took place, at which the circumstances surrounding the two deaths were explained. At the conclusion of the inquest, the foreman said that the jury wished unanimously to express their admiration of the courageous conduct of the superintendent, late sergeant and two constables. They also donated their fees to the fund set up to raise money for Molden's family.

The chairman of the magistrates closed that hearing by saying that the sergeant would soon have been entitled to a pension, which he richly deserved given his distinguished career. To loud applause from within the packed court, he committed the accused to Devizes Gaol to await his trial and added:

> 'We all know the risks the police run and how zealously they perform their duties at all times. If this poor man had been spared, he would, as I have already said, received most probably this pension and it is most sad and deplorable to think that life should have been so flagrantly taken away. I would only add that I feel sure we all appreciate the manner in which the police have concluded this case from the commencement'

In May, in recognition of the courageous behaviour of his officers in arresting Gurd, the Chief Constable presented Superintendent Perrett with £10 and Constable Davies and the newly promoted Sergeant Langley with £3 each. Furthermore, in early July, the committee formed to collect funds for the murdered officer's family announced that £985 had been raised.

On Monday 11 July, Gurd appeared at the Wiltshire Summer Assizes to face trial for the murder of Henry Richards only and entered a guilty plea. It was only with the greatest difficulty that the trial judge persuaded him to plead not guilty and his trial took place the following day. Although no evidence of insanity was offered by the defence, his barrister suggested to the jury that as Gurd had spent so much time with lunatics, he may have been temporarily insane at the time both murders took place. However, having listened to the evidence, which was similar to that given at the preliminary hearings, the jury rejected this and convicted him

James Billington, the hangman. (The author)

of wilful murder. As the judge was sentencing him to death, Florence, who was sitting in the ladies' gallery, burst into tears.

The condemned man was executed on Tuesday 26 July by hangman James Billington. He had weighed Gurd beforehand and on learning he was a little over nine stones, he allowed a drop of six feet and ten inches and death was instantaneous.

The constable was buried in the town's Minster on the Saturday following his murder. Many of his former comrades were present together with several hundred local residents and members of his family, among them his four sons. The coffin was strewn with flowers provided by the Marchioness of Bath. Eight months later, towards the end of December, a memorial stone was placed on his grave, bearing this inscription:

'In memory of Enos Molden, police sergeant in the Wilts Constabulary, who, on the morning of the 12th April 1892, while assisting in the apprehension of John Gurd, then charged with and after convicted of wilful murder of Henry Richards of Melksham, was shot dead by the murderer at a spot on the Corsley

Road, near Longleat Gate. This memorial was erected by the chief constable, superintendents, officers and constables of the Wilts Constabulary, in recognition of the gallant conduct of their brother officer, who had been for thirty-two years in the force and was respected by everyone who knew him.'

20

Detective Sergeant Joseph Joyce
Metropolitan Police
1892

In the summer of 1892, 25-year-old George Wenzel was working for fellow German, Henry Selzer, a baker with premises on Haggerston Road, Dalston in London, where both men also lived. However, Wenzel found alternative employment and on 13 June started work for Frederick Ruman, a German butcher, whose shop was at 81, Charing Cross Road. Wenzel moved in with his new employer at 176, Sandringham Buildings, supposedly on a temporary basis, until he found accommodation of his own.

A few days later, on the 19th, Wenzel paid a social visit to Herr Selzer and the two men chatted for some time. After Wenzel left, his former employer realised that a cashbox containing documents and £9 in notes was missing and he visited the local police station to report the matter. It was arranged that Detective Sergeant Joseph Joyce would visit him the next day and when the officer arrived, the baker told him of his suspicions and the two of them set off for the butcher's shop on Charing Cross Road to confront Wenzel. However, he was not there and after waiting for some time, the sergeant, accompanied by Herr Ruman, went in search of him. A short time later, they met him on the street and returned with him to the butcher's shop, the detective having now identified himself as a police officer.

When told he was suspected of stealing the cash and papers, Wenzel denied having done so. However, the sergeant insisted on searching his bedroom and as the four men made their way there, Herr Ruman mentioned that three or four days earlier, he had noticed that his watch and chain had gone missing. However, he had not noticed that his revolver had also been taken from the place he usually kept it. A search of Wenzel's room proved fruitless and the sergeant went into the kitchen, where he saw a portmanteau belonging to Wenzel and when opened, the stolen papers were found. A search was then made of his clothing, which led to the discovery of the £9 in cash and the watch.

Joyce advised Wenzel he was arresting him on suspicion of theft, but as he took out his handcuffs, Wenzel produced what turned out to be his employer's revolver, which he pointed first of all at the sergeant and then at the two other men. Several shots rang out in rapid succession, the first of which hit the sergeant and the others wounded Herren Selzer and Ruman. The sergeant fell to the floor, shouting as he did so, 'He has shot me and got loose.' Herr Selzer grappled with Wenzel and managed to take the revolver from him as Herr Ruman ran from the room in search of help. Wenzel was by now hysterical, screaming repeatedly, 'I am going to die, I am going to die,' as he was dragged out into the corridor.

Detective Sergeant Thomas Bowden had rooms in the Sandringham Buildings, which were nearby and was off duty at home. He heard what he recognised to be gunfire and taking hold

Wenzel shoots Detective Sergeant Joyce. (The Illustrated Police News)

140

of his truncheon, went to investigate. He met Herr Ruman, who was shouting, 'Police, murder,' and shortly afterwards they were able to subdue Wenzel. Moments later, several police officers, who had been told of the incident, arrived and helped to take him to Vine Street Police Station, where a carton containing forty-four cartridges was found in his pockets. These matched one found at the scene of the shooting and those removed from the wounds suffered by the sergeant and the two other men. They were taken .to Charing Cross Hospital, where bullets were removed from Herr Selzer's left arm and from the back of Herr Ruman's head. Their wounds proved to be superficial and neither man suffered lasting damage. The sergeant had been shot in the stomach and right arm, the first of which was the more serious. The bullet had penetrated his left kidney and the left lobe of his liver, which a post-mortem would later show had caused him to bleed to death.

It was hoped that a deathbed deposition could be taken from him and later that afternoon, a local magistrate was standing at his bedside. He told him, 'Now Joyce, you are in a dangerous state, tell us how you met with your injuries.' In a weak voice, he made the following reply, 'I was trying to catch a thief and was shot by the prisoner.' He died moments later so that it proved impossible to take a legally acceptable deposition from him. Wenzel had been taken to the hospital in the hope the sergeant would have been able to formally identify him as his killer, but he died before this could be done. When Wenzel was asked if he agreed to attend the hospital for this purpose, he did so readily, saying, 'Yes, to ask his forgiveness.'

The accused man was engaged to a young German woman, Lena Kohler, who was working as a domestic servant in Canonbury and two days after the shooting, she received the following letter, dated the 21 June from Wenzel, who was in Holloway Prison and

George Wenzel. (The Illustrated Police News)

in which he suggests he had not been told of the sergeant's death although he realised he probably would die of his wounds. It was written in German and Lena handed it to the police, who arranged for it to be translated:

'Dear Cousin Lena, Fear and trembling will come over you, for if I had been in Germany I could never have become what I have become in London – namely a criminal. Oh heaven! What have I done to become so quickly a thief and a murderer? But it is all an aberration of mind that has visited me suddenly. I am not always clear in my mind and that was the case on Monday last, when I wrote a letter to you, in which you will observe my absence of mind. After not being the whole of the afternoon at Selzer's, I took away in the evening a cash-box and several things belonging to Mr Ruman, my master. I did no longer lodge where I did lodge the first few days because some of my money had been stolen there. I then lodged at the business premises upstairs, next to my master's room.

'Well, Monday morning came and I had something to do in town. When I returned at two in the afternoon, Mr Selzer and a detective were present there to arrest me. I went upstairs with them, to the sitting-room at 81 Charing Cross Road, a German sausage and provision shop. When we were upstairs Mr Ruman also came there. They searched about and found everything I had stolen. I do not know where my things are at the present moment. I had 33 shillings in money and some German money and when the detective was going to secure my hands and take my revolver, I fired on him. He is very severely injured and they say possibly going to die. Selzer has been wounded in the arm and Ruman in the head, yet I could not liberate myself. I was taken to prison.

'Oh, dearest angel. Pardon me! Most certainly I shall have to die. Oh Lena dear, go to the Queen of England! Tell her your grief, tell her of my mental disease and beg for mercy. Also go to the German Consul. Oh, cannot you help me once more? Write to me at once so that I shall know whether you have received these lines. I am your G. WENZEL. Come and see me next Sunday, perhaps we may be allowed to speak together. If I had my liberty I would return to my home. On Tuesday 28th June, I shall have to appear before the Magistrate.'

The letter was important to the crown in its case, when Wenzel's trial opened at the Old Bailey on 25 July, for in it he admitted the thefts and the shootings. His claim that the shootings were accidental and occurred when he was temporarily insane was rejected by the jury, who found him guilty of wilful murder. He was sentenced to death and given the seriousness of the crime, a petition seeking a reprieve, based on his youth, was rejected.

He was executed at Newgate Prison on 16 August and it was a double hanging. Standing at his side on the drop was 60-year-old James Taylor, a decorated hero of the Crimean War, who had been convicted of murdering his wife.

21

Sergeant Michael Rogan
Royal Irish Constabulary
1892

As the nineteenth century was drawing to a close, the police barrack in Ballinadrimna, County Kildare, was a whitewashed two storey building, which usually housed a sergeant and three constables. However, in late October 1892, one constable was transferred out of the district and another was taken ill and admitted to the hospital in Edenderry. The officers remaining in post there were Sergeant Michael Rogan and Constable John Pilkington, a 28-year-old single man.

The 38-year-old sergeant was married and his family was also living in the barrack. These were his wife Rebecca, eleven years his junior and their seven children, Elizabeth (12), Rebecca (10), George (9), Helena (7), Lucy (5), James (3) and Michael (1).

The sergeant had been stationed in Ballinadrimna for eight years and the constable for four and police colleagues believed the men to be on friendly terms. The Rogans and the constable took an active part in village life and were respected and popular with their neighbours. Such was the apparent strength of their relationship that Pilkington was godfather of James and Michael and the sergeant had recommended him for promotion. The events which occurred in the early hours of Friday 1 November therefore came as a great shock to everyone who knew them.

Mary Kelly was employed as a domestic servant at the barrack and as usual, she arrived at eight o'clock that morning to start her duties. She was surprised to find the back door locked and that there was no response when she called out to those inside. She gained entry through the front door, to discover the building was full of smoke and small fires were burning in several of the rooms.

She ran to the bedroom, in which the sergeant, his wife and all their children slept to ensure they were all well, but the smoke was so thick, she could see nothing. She made for Mrs Rogan's bed but was unable to rouse her. She then heard Elizabeth call to her in a weak voice and taking hold of her, ran in search of the constable for help, but could not find him. Still holding on to the youngster, Mary ran from the building. Three men heard her shouting for help and soon extinguished the fires. One of them had made his way upstairs and on rejoining the others, looking stunned, he said in a low voice, 'There's murder here.'

It was obvious that the fires had been started deliberately with paraffin and whiskey, which had been poured over clothing, beds and furniture in every room. An initial search of the barrack led to the discovery of the bodies of Sergeant Rogan and his wife, lying side by side in their bed, their faces covered in blood having apparently been shot. All of the children had suffered terrible injuries to their heads and faces, which were horribly bruised and swollen. Rebecca and Lucy were dead and the surviving children were removed to the homes of neighbours to await medical attention, although they were given no hope of surviving. Pilkington's fully clothed body was in his bedroom. He was lying on the floor in front of the fireplace. He had suffered a massive head wound and a revolver, issued by the police, was close to his right hand and five of its six chambers were empty. His wig had been dislodged and lay several inches from his head.

Details of what had occurred were to emerge a few days later, when two inquests were held at the barrack. The first was in respect of the sergeant and his family members, which now included James, who died later on the day of the tragedy; the other focused on Pilkington's death. Given the traumatic events Elizabeth had lived through, she was not required to attend the hearing and her account of what happened after the family went to bed at ten o'clock on the night of the tragedy, was read out by a police officer. She woke up in the middle of the night when somebody entered the bedroom and lit a match. She realised it was Pilkington, who said nothing as he made for her parents' bed. There was a gunshot and she heard her mother scream out, 'That's a shot,' but she fell silent after more shots rang out.

Pilkington then turned on the children, beating each of them about the head with a truncheon, causing very serious injuries. Elizabeth was aware at least two had run from the room before he grabbed hold of her and as he was hitting her, screamed 'Are you mad too?' He stopped suddenly and left, giving her the opportunity to lock the door. However, shortly afterwards he smashed the door open and resumed the beatings, the severity of which became evident when three broken truncheons were later discovered at the scene. He left the room and a terrified Elizabeth kept quiet and hid, fearing he would return, but he did not do so.

Before details of the post mortems were given, the hearing was provided with progress reports on the other surviving children. Helena had shown signs of recovery and she was allowed to sit in a chair, but her condition had deteriorated and she was returned to her bed; neither George nor Michael had regained consciousness and it was thought unlikely that the two boys would survive for much longer.

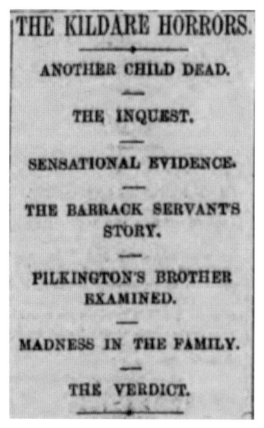

The tragic events at Ballinadrimna received widespread publicity. (The Freeman's Journal)

Dr John Robinson of Johnstownbridge carried out post mortems on all of the deceased and gave details of his findings. Sergeant Rogan was shot once, through the right eye and the bullet had lodged in his brain and he must have died instantaneously. Mrs Rogan was also shot through the right eye and the bullet had exited below her left ear; part of her face had been destroyed by a second bullet and in her case also, death was instantaneous. Rebecca, Lucy and James were not shot; all suffered fractured skulls and their injuries were consistent with having been beaten with a truncheon.

The inquest into the constable's death was then opened and details were given of Pilkington's movements on the eve of the killings. He visited Mr Dowling's public house in the village, where he met a friend, who noticed nothing unusual in his behaviour. He bemoaned the fact that he was poorly educated but otherwise appeared cheerful and happy with his situation. He left at nine thirty and insisted on shaking his friend's hand, which he had never done before. He had drunk just two bottles of porter and two small glasses of whiskey and was sober.

Dr Robinson had also examined Pilkington's body and advised the court that one bullet had entered at the right temple, passed through the brain and came out just above his left ear. It was undoubtedly self-inflicted and he used the revolver found at his side. The doctor added that he believed it possible that Pilkington had suffered from epilepsy, which if known to his superiors would have led to his being compelled to resign. However, there was nothing to suggest this had any bearing on the tragedy. It was left to Pilkington's brother Patrick, who knew nothing of a history of epilepsy, to provide one possible explanation for what had happened. He advised the court that his brother had never shown any signs of mental instability although an aunt and a great-uncle had been confined in a lunatic asylum.

Constable John Pilkington.
(The author)

In his summing up, the coroner advised the jury that there was no rational explanation for what had happened that night. Both men were Catholics and there was no history of antagonism, indeed the opposite was true. He believed that on returning to the barrack, Pilkington brooded in his room for two or three hours, before becoming demented. Seizing the revolver and truncheons, he rushed to the Rogans' bedroom, shooting first of all the sleeping sergeant and then his half-awake wife. He then attacked the children, after which he ran from room to room, setting the fires, before returning to his room, where he shot himself. The jury agreed and after a few minutes returned with the widely predicted verdict, that whilst temporarily insane, Pilkington murdered the sergeant, his wife and the children, before committing suicide.

The sergeant was a native of County Louth and had served in the police for fifteen years, the first seven of which were spent in Cork. This was the birthplace of his wife and was where they met. However, they had lived happily in Ballinadrimna for eight years and the village was where their children regarded as home. The families of Sergeant and Mrs Rogan therefore decided they and their dead children should be buried in the village.

At noon, on the Thursday following the murders, a large crowd gathered outside the barrack and watched in silence as the five coffins emerged. That containing the sergeant was carried by four other sergeants and that of his wife by four constables. Those of James, Lucy and Rebecca were carried by a number of village children. They were taken to the nearby church, where in the graveyard there was a plot known as The Stranger's Home, which was reserved for those not born in the district and it was here that two graves were prepared. In one, the coffins of the parents were lowered and in the other, the coffins of the children were placed. Pilkington's body had been taken to Phillipstown, his birth place, which was where he was interred. Apart from members of his immediate family, there were very few mourners.

Over the following weeks, the surviving children were taken to the National Children's Hospital in Dublin, where they made good progress. They were then sent to live with their paternal grandparents in County Louth.

22

Acting Sergeant Adam Eves
Essex Constabulary
1893

Acting Sergeant Adam Eves of the Essex Constabulary, based at Maldon, walked into the Oak Inn at Hazeleigh at ten o'clock on the night of Saturday 15 April 1893. There had been a number of incidents of rook poisoning throughout the district in the recent past, a practice prohibited by the Poisoned Grain Act of 1863. He left a notice offering a reward of ten shillings for anyone who provided information leading to the arrests of those responsible, which the landlord agreed to display in the bar. The sergeant was nearing the end of his shift at eleven-thirty, but when he did not return home, his wife was not worried unduly. She had always known him to be a conscientious officer, committed to helping those living in the area and believed he had probably remained on duty to assist colleagues with a serious incident of some description. Sadly, she would learn the following day, the reason why he did not come home.

Acting Sergeant Adam John Eves.
(The Illustrated Police News)

Mrs Eves not having raised the alarm and given that he was not due to report for duty the next day, Eves had not been reported missing by three o'clock the following

149

afternoon, when local carpenter, Herbert Patten was walking through a field. He noticed a large amount of blood on the ground, causing him to peer into a ditch which was close by and was horrified to discover the officer's body, immersed in several inches of water. Herbert raised the alarm and fortunately, Inspector C.E. Pryke was at the neighbouring Hazeleigh Hall Farm, from which the recent theft of a large quantity of corn had been reported. The inspector made his way to where the body lay and found it to be cold and stiff, indicating Eves had been dead for some time and he realised that his colleague had been severely beaten before his throat was slashed.

The sergeant's body was taken to his home, where a post mortem was performed by a local doctor, George Scott, who was able to say that he had been dead for at least twelve hours and that all of the injuries were confined to the head and throat. The left eye was swollen and closed and there were many injuries to the head. There were three wounds to the forehead and two to the side of the head, some of which had exposed the skull and all were caused by a blunt instrument. He was also able to state that a knife was used to inflict two wounds near his left ear. There were three distinct knife wounds to the throat, the most serious of which had been the cause of death. It started at the left ear and ran around the edge of the jaw to the right ear, damaging the root of the tongue and divided all the main vessels and muscles, before cutting the vertebral column.

The dead officer, who was married but had no children, was a wheelwright in his youth, before joining the Essex Constabulary in 1877. He had served in Southend, Witham and Harwich before being transferred to Maldon in 1891. He was promoted to acting sergeant the previous April and was expected to rise through the ranks. He was commended on several occasions, once for his prompt action which led to the arrests of a gang of fowl stealers, all of whom were sentenced to four months hard labour. He also distinguished himself by solving a serious case of chaff theft and he had been seriously injured when arresting a poacher. He was a member of the St John Ambulance Association and had been called upon to use his first-aid skills on numerous occasions to help colleagues, members of the public and offenders.

THE FIRST JOURNEY.

It was believed the murdered officer had interrupted thieves at Hazeleigh Hall Farm. (The Illustrated Police News)

His commitment to the police and the public he served were common knowledge and the sense of initial loss and anger felt throughout the district was heightened when it was learnt of events earlier on the Saturday, his last day on duty. At about noon, he saw an elderly woman, who lived alone, fall to the ground in her front garden. He rushed over, lifted her up, took her indoors and ensured she was not badly injured, before promising to return later that day. He did so two hours later and sat with her for a while. Before leaving, he told her that his mother was due to visit him in the near future and he would bring her to call when she did so. Of course, such a visit would not now take place.

A search of the murder scene led to the discovery of three heavy sticks, which it was believed were used to strike the deceased. Also, three sacks of wheat were found on the ground close to the body and another three in a nearby pond, all apparently abandoned in haste by the attackers. The officers investigating the crime believed that at some time between ten and eleven o'clock on Saturday night, Eves

The murder. (The Illustrated Police News)

had come across at least three men in the process of stealing sacks of wheat from the barn at Hazeleigh Hall Farm and had challenged them. His truncheon had not been drawn so it was thought he was set upon immediately and had little chance of defending himself. After being beaten to the ground with the sticks, his throat was cut. Given the nature of the theft, the culprits would have had to have had a cart, in which they had made their escape.

Captain Edward Showers, the Chief Constable of Essex, received the following telegraph advising him of the crime:

'Sergeant Eves murdered at Hazeleigh Saturday night while endeavouring to arrest corn stealers. Body found this afternoon. Frightfully mutilated. Six sacks corn found close by. No arrests at present.'

The body is discovered. (The Illustrated Police News)

However, it would not be long before arrests were made. It was known that Eves had for some time suspected a group of local men to be responsible of stealing sacks of wheat from farms in the area and his enquiries had led to threats being made against him. He had given details to his senior officers, which meant the investigation into his murder, very quickly focused on this group. Furthermore, when news of the murder became more widely known, villagers came forward with details of threats they had heard made against him and two names in particular were prominent.

James Ramsey Snr had reportedly threatened Eves on many occasions and one informant had heard him say he would not give him a chance if he interrupted him committing a crime and would 'Knock him right down at once'. Another villager had heard him say that he kept a large stick in his cart and would use it against the constable. Also of great significance was the information that another man, John

James Ramsey the elder. (The Illustrated Police News)

Davis, was heard as recently as Saturday evening say of Eves 'I'll kill that bugger if he comes where I am tonight'.

Within a matter of hours, six men were arrested and these were John Davis (34), his brother Richard (30) and their brother-in-law Charles Sales (47), together with James Ramsey (38), his son also James (15) and their friend John Bateman (37). All were casual farm labourers and except for Bateman, who said he was sleeping rough in Woodham Mortimer, all claimed to have been at home with their families at the time the murder was thought to have taken place. Despite the suspects denying they were involved in the crime, the police nevertheless believed they had sufficient evidence to charge them.

When the clothes of the arrested men were examined, what were believed to be blood stains were found on some of them. However, John Davis insisted those on his outer garments were tea stains and those inside his coat pockets were from a hare he had trapped a few days earlier. A mark was found on the back of his brother's coat, which Richard could not explain, but said it was not blood. The brothers owned a cart and there appeared to be spots of blood in it, which John explained were from a sheep's head his wife had bought recently and which she placed in the cart. There was also a cart track from near the ditch in which the body had been thrown and this led to within a few yards of the cottage of Richard Davis. He admitted the track was caused by his cart, but he said he had been picking up stones. There was only a very small mark on a pair of the older Ramsey's trousers, but a search of his house revealed a pile of recently washed clothes belonging to him and his son, which suggested they had attempted to get rid of any incriminating stains. As for Sales, he claimed a mark to the front of his waistcoat was the blood from a piece of meat he had eaten and one on the back was already there when he bought it from a friend.

The half dozen sacks, believed to have been abandoned by the killers when disturbed by the sergeant, all bore the trader's name, 'Ingleden, Davonport. Borough Market'. Eleven similar sacks were concealed in different rooms of the Ramseys' home and also in the house of the Davis brothers' parents. Some of these sacks contained traces of corn, barley and peas, which the suspects claimed were grown in a field owned by the brothers' father. However, the police were satisfied after talking to farmers in the area that the field in question had not been cultivated for at least four years. Furthermore, local millers came forward to say that for some time the Davis brothers had regularly brought them wheat, barley and other crops to be ground. As far as the police were concerned, the sacks supported their belief in the culpability of the arrested men. All of this physical evidence, together with some hair which was clasped in the sergeant's hand, was sent to Dr Thomas Stevenson, lecturer in Medical Jurisprudence at Guy's Hospital in London for analysis.

The Davis brothers and the Ramseys were working at Hazeleigh Hall Farm on the days before the murder and it was believed they had threshed more corn than they had told the farmer. They planned to steal the excess amount with the help of Bateman and Sales, on the Saturday night, believing nobody would realise that the theft had taken place It was now thought probable they had committed similar crimes when working on other local farms in the past.

As the investigation progressed, it became clear that there was no evidence against Bateman and at a hearing before local magistrates, he was discharged. However, he did not simply walk out of the courtroom, for he entered the witness box to testify on behalf of the crown. He told the hushed court that on 24 April, while on remand in Chelmsford Gaol, he asked Sales who was to represent him in court and his reply was that it was pointless having a solicitor as he was guilty. He continued by accusing the Davis brothers of also being guilty. This led to an angry outburst by the three men from the dock, saying he had concocted the story in an attempt to save himself.

James Ramsey Junior.
(The Illustrated Police News)

The police also produced another witness, Thomas Choat, a casual labourer who had been feeding the thresher used by the Ramseys on the day of the murder. He stated that he had seen the older Ramsey and John Davis deep in conversation and apparently attempting to ensure nobody overheard them, but he did hear them say they would meet later that night. Again, both men shouted from the dock that he was lying and acting out of revenge as he and the older Ramsey had argued in the recent past.

Meanwhile, little time was lost in finding a replacement for Eves, following his funeral in Purleigh, the Saturday after his death. Constable A.C. Cowell had joined the force seven years earlier and during that time, served in Terling, Canewdon and Purleigh. He had a reputation for bravery and had once, single-handedly, taken a gun from a dangerous offender. It was decided that he should be armed with a revolver on taking up his new post, given the murder of his predecessor. A precedent had been set some years earlier when officers responsible for policing Epping Forest were armed as there had been a spate of desperate confrontations with gangs of horse thieves in that area.

The final hearings before the coroner and magistrates in respect of Eves were delayed until Dr Stevenson had completed his analysis of the items sent to him. His testimony to both courts was eagerly anticipated but proved to be something of an anti-climax. He stated that he had examined all of the stains sent to him and was able to confirm most were mammalian blood, but the quantities were so small that he could not determine if they were animal or human. He was therefore unable to undermine the explanations given for the stains on their clothes by the accused men. As for the hair clasped in the sergeant's hand, he could not say with any certainty, that it matched any of the samples he had taken from the accused. He had also examined some knives discovered by the police but could not identify the murder weapon.

Having listened to the doctor, the coroner's jury found that Eves was:

> 'Foully murdered by some person or persons unknown, but at the same time we consider that very grave suspicion attaches to the prisoners, but we do not think the evidence at present is quite sufficient to commit, We hope the police will continue in their endeavours to throw additional light upon the crime'.

The magistrates decided there was no evidence against young Ramsey, who was discharged but there was against his father, the Davis brothers and Sales, who were all committed to stand trial for murder at the next Essex Assizes.

A fund was opened on behalf of the sergeant's widow and in excess of £400 was raised, with donations coming from many constabularies throughout the country and many smaller donations from local people. Mrs Eves was also granted an annual police pension of £15 and when the fund was closed, £350 was invested to provide her with her an annuity of £23 17s 2d. However, sympathy was not reserved for Mrs Eves alone and on 9 June the *Chelmsford Chronicle* published the following letter:

> 'SIR, glad as I am that a goodly sum has been secured to the widow of the late P S Eves, who was so cruelly done to death, I am also glad to hear that a fund is being started for the relief of the wives and children of the men suspected of that crime. That they are in distress cannot be denied. I trust that a sum may be raised to prevent at least the innocent wives and children suffering and that some means may be found to prevent them from becoming members of the submerged tenth. The Rev D I Preston of Latchington has undertaken the receipt of any sums that may be sent for their relief and I hope the list will be a substantial one. I enclose my card. MIDDLE TEMPLE'

The appeal met with some success and £212 was collected for the families of the accused.

The trial of the four men opened on 27 July and in their opening statement, the crown acknowledged that Sales was not working at Hazeleigh Hall Farm on the day of the murder with the three other accused and conceded there was little evidence against him. No additional evidence other than that given at the preliminary hearings was produced during the trial, but the crown made much of the fact that no witnesses were called to provide alibis for the prisoners. The jury found the Davis brothers guilty and they were sentenced to death; the other two defendants were cleared of any involvement although a jury member later told of a belief by some who sat with him that the older Ramsey was heavily involved in the murder but there was insufficient evidence to convict him.

Those misgivings soon proved to have been justified. Shortly after the trial came to an end, Lena Davis visited her husband John in the condemned cell at Chelmsford Gaol and he told her of the events of the day of the murder. He had already given a statement to the prison governor and encouraged Lena to advise the press of his account.

According to Davis, the theft was planned by Ramsey Snr, who on the Saturday afternoon offered the brothers ten shillings each to help him remove the sacks and both agreed to do so. On the night, the three of them were in the process of stealing the sacks of corn, when the sergeant confronted John and believing him to be alone, said 'Hallo Jack, what's your game? I'm going to provide you with a bed tonight'. Richard was some distance ahead and could not have known what was happening, but Ramsey left the barn and crept up on the officer from behind. He struck Eves with a large stick which stunned him and the three men struggled for twenty minutes. Eventually, Eves was overpowered and as John held him down, Ramsey slashed his throat. Richard, who had not been involved in the attack now returned to the scene and was horrified to see the body. John concluded by telling Lena he could have spared Richard from being implicated in the crime as an accessory, but John had begged him to remain silent in the hope that he might eventually be found not guilty.

John's attempt to provide grounds for a reprieve for his brother proved to be successful and Richard was instead sentenced to penal servitude for life. When told the news, John said, 'I'm very glad, it's the right thing.' He was hanged by James Billington on the morning of 16 August and was buried later that day in the prison grounds.

News of Ramsey's alleged leading role in the murder provoked a public outcry, which intensified when it was realised he could not be tried for the same crime a second time. However, five days before John's execution, Ramsey was arrested and charged with the theft of thirteen and a half bushels of corn from Hazeleigh Hall Farm on the night of 15 April. He pleaded not guilty on his appearance at the November Assizes, when the chief prosecution witness was Richard Davis. Ramsey was convicted of the crime and there was loud cheering in the public gallery when the judge sentenced him to fourteen years penal servitude.

23

Sub-Inspector James Allan
Lanarkshire Constabulary
1893

Late on the night of 4 September 1893, a man approached Sub-Inspector James Allan and Constable John Pirrie, who were standing on Inchbelly Road in Bishopbriggs, four miles from the centre of Glasgow. He advised them of a crime in progress a short distance away, as two men were taking clothes and valuables from a drunk who had collapsed outside the Crow Tavern.

As the officers ran towards the scene, they encountered two suspicious looking characters coming from the direction of the public house. They were stopped but insisted they knew nothing of any offence. The officers did not believe them and the sub-inspector grabbed hold of one by the collar, who was later identified as William Coubrough and the constable took hold of the other man in a similar manner, who was Richard Magee. The four men set off for the Crow Tavern, the sub-inspector and Coubrough, a few yards ahead of the other pair. Suddenly, Coubrough tried to break free, leading to a brief struggle and the constable watched in horror as his comrade fell to the ground, shouting, 'I'm stabbed.' The suspect then ran off across nearby fields in the direction of Glasgow.

He was lying in the middle of the road and the constable asked two young men who were nearby, to help but they refused to become involved. Pirrie therefore decided to take Magee to the Bishopbriggs Police Office, where he was thrown unceremoniously into a cell without his details being taken or a search of him being made.

It was five minutes later that Pirrie returned to the scene of the stabbing and from the blood trail he could see that the wounded officer

MURDER OF A POLICE INSPECTOR

The murder. (The Illustrated Police News)

had attempted to give chase to his assailant but growing weaker, he had staggered to the footpath. He was lying in a massive pool of blood and whispered, 'I am dying,' and moments later he stopped breathing. The constable carried the corpse to the sub-inspector's cottage, which was not far away, where he had to raise Mrs Allan from her bed to give her the terrible news.

The senior officers of the Lanarkshire Constabulary were alerted and an order issued that a thorough search of the scene should be made. The weapon used was discovered, which was a clasp knife stained with blood. It was learnt from the drunken victim of the robbery that ten shillings, a clasp knife and his top coat had been stolen from him.

When Magee, a 38-year-old miner of no fixed address, was removed from the cell at the police office for questioning, it was discovered he was in possession of the drunk's own clasp knife, which had therefore not been used in the stabbing. Now aware of the very serious situation he was in, he decided to co-operate and made the following statement, in which he named Coubrough as his companion:

> 'On Monday 4th September about half-past nine or ten o'clock, I left Glasgow to go to Kilsyth with William Coubrough, whom I had previously known at Bishopbriggs. We saw a man lying on the footway. I was at the time a little behind Coubrough. I did not touch him nor did I see Coubrough touch him. A short distance further on the way we met two policemen. They asked if we had seen anyone on the road. I said "Yes, we saw a man on the footpath". They told us to go back. One of them took hold of me and the other took hold of Coubrough. We had only gone a few yards when a struggle took place between the policeman and Coubrough and during the scuffle I heard the policemen cry "I am stabbed" and saw him fall. Coubrough ran away. Then I was taken to the police office and locked up.'

A native of Camprie, Coubrough was 42 years old, single and a miner. He was well known to the police as he had been sentenced to five years penal servitude on 12 September 1888 at the Glasgow Circuit Court for carrying out a burglary of the Broomhill Convalescent Home. He was a ticket-of-leave man, who had not reported to the police on release as he was required to do and was therefore already a wanted man. Coubrough's description was circulated, giving his height as five feet five inches. It also listed his many tattoos; on his chest there was a sailing ship and a woman in chains; on his right arm there was an eagle, several flags, a crown, horse, bracelet and harp; on his left arm, hand and wrist could be found an anchor, heart, shamrock and a number of other flags surrounding a crown.

A post-mortem revealed that the sub-inspector, who was 50 years old when he died, had been stabbed in the back, but death resulted from another far more serious stab wound to the groin. An artery had been severed which had led to a massive loss of blood. He was buried on the afternoon of Friday 8 September with full honours. Born and raised in Newarthill, he had initially served in the Renfrewshire Constabulary for one year before joining the Lanarkshire force in February 1870. He served with distinction and transferred to Bishopbriggs in July 1882 as a sub-inspector. He left a widow and eight children, some of whom were adults, one of his daughters being a teacher at Auchinairn.

Despite four days of searching, Coubrough remained at large and on the day of the interment, officers of the Lanarkshire and Stirlingshire forces, assisted by a number of gamekeepers and villagers, had searched the district around Blairtummock but without success. However, it was decided to make another sweep of the area and a group of officers led by Sub-Inspector Moir began to search the outhouses of a farm. The fugitive was discovered asleep in a hayshed and when woken up, he acknowledged who he was and surrendered without presenting any difficulties. He was tired and hungry and seemed almost relieved to be taken into custody. He recognised the sub-inspector, asking, 'Is that you Moir? I'm glad to see you but not on such an occasion as this.'

The party arrived at the Glasgow Central Police Office, in a borrowed horse drawn cart at ten minutes past six and having been placed in a cell, Coubrough's only request was for something to eat. He was charged with Sub-Inspector Allan's murder and after a brief court appearance, he was remanded into custody at Duke Street Prison. As he awaited his trial, he received the news that his mother, who had been taken ill when she first learnt of the killing, had died following his arrest. Those who knew her were convinced she had died of shame.

Coubrough appeared alone, before trial judge Lord Young in the High Court of Judiciary on 30 October, but by this time, his barrister, Mr Crabbe Watt and the public prosecutor had agreed that he would not face a charge of murder and that he would be permitted to plead guilty to culpable homicide. Coubrough's account of the crime had been accepted reluctantly as the prosecution believed it would have difficulty to contradict him.

He described heading for Kilsyth with Magee, when they came across the drunk lying barely conscious on the road. Giving way to temptation, they stole a number of items from him. Afterwards, Coubrough had taken out his clasp knife to cut some tobacco and at this moment, they were challenged by the police officers. As they were being taken back to where the drunk was lying, he attempted to break free and as he did so, the accidental stabbing occurred as Allan

Lord Young, the trial judge.
(The author)

fell against the open knife. Mr Crabbe Watt told the court that his client, who spent the hearing with his head bowed, had been in a state of mental agony as he recognised he was responsible for two deaths, that of the police officer and of his mother.

Lord Young made his displeasure known to the public prosecutor, commenting, 'Surely this case ought to go to trial.' Nevertheless, he was advised once again that the plea was considered appropriate. The judge replied he would retire to consider the matter further. On his return to the courtroom he confirmed that he would agree to the charge of culpable homicide, albeit reluctantly.

Turning to Coubrough, Lord Young told him the prosecution had been extremely merciful but this was an exceptionally serious case, concerning the brutal death of a police officer performing his duty. He had considered a life sentence but had pulled back and sentenced him to penal servitude for ten years.

24

Constable James Gordon
Lancashire Constabulary
1893

Constable James Gordon was one of eight children and grew up on a farm in Kirkandineshire. In the summer of 1888 he decided to travel south and subsequently joined the St Helens Police Force. Five years later, as midnight approached on Sunday 12 November 1893, the 26-year-old officer was on duty with his colleague, Constable John Whalley and as they passed Foster's Navigation Boiler Works, they noticed that the windows of the hen cote, which was situated in the yard of the foundry, had been smashed. Suspecting a break-in was taking place, they decided to investigate. On entering, Whalley raised his lamp to reveal two men were inside and on the floor there were two hens, the heads of which had very recently been removed.

The intruders were 32-year-old Frank Riley and John Carney who was 19 years of age. The lamp was kicked from Whalley's hand, but he managed to take hold of Carney and Gordon grabbed Riley. As the four men fought, Riley delivered a terrific punch to Gordon's chest which left him struggling to breathe and unsteady on his feet. Nevertheless, he and Whalley were able to drag the two men towards the door, but as they emerged into the yard, Whalley was struck a severe blow to his back and this was by a brick thrown by a third man, twenty-two year old John Leahey. Carney and Riley freed themselves and as they were doing so, Leahey hit Gordon on the head with an iron bar, which was one of several lying on the ground, as a result of which Gordon suffered a serious head wound.

The three men now began to throw stones, which were scattered about the yard, hitting the officers a number of times and after a few minutes, Leahey took the opportunity to climb over the roof of the

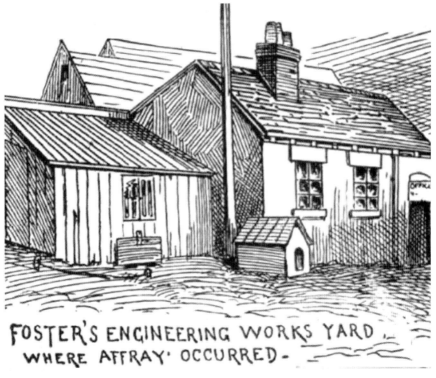

FOSTER'S ENGINEERING WORKS YARD,
WHERE AFFRAY OCCURRED.

The scene of the suspected break-in, investigated by Constables Gordon and Whalley. (The Illustrated Police News)

foundry and clear of the premises. By now, Whalley had his staff in his hand and used it to strike Carney who fell to the ground, but Riley was also able to flee the scene. The officers set off for the St Helens Police Station with their prisoner, but Carney was in no mood to cooperate and put up a fierce resistance. On one occasion, Gordon was forced to kneel on the pavement and Carney took the opportunity to kick him on the head and a large amount of blood started to flow from the wound. When they eventually arrived at the station, Gordon wrote a report on the night's events in which he noted that he had been hit by Riley in the hen cote, struck on the head with an iron bar by Leahey and kicked on the head by Carney.

His three assailants were colliers and had not worked for some time as they were on strike and it was presumed that the motive for the break in was simply to provide food for themselves and their families. As there had been a number of violent confrontations involving the police and striking miners it was thought this explained their aggressive response when approached by Gordon and Whalley. However, they were no strangers to the local police court. Leahey had the lengthiest history of convictions, having appeared on twenty occasions for offences of theft, assault and drunkenness; Riley, the only one of them who was married, had twenty previous convictions for matters of vagrancy, drunkenness, burglary and police assault; Carney had made eight appearances for theft and acts of violence.

Constable James Gordon. (The author)

Whalley's back injury was quite minor and did not require much attention from Dr McNichol, the local police surgeon who had been asked to attend the station. Gordon, on the other hand, had suffered what appeared to be minor injuries to his body, but also two serious wounds to his head. One of these was one and a half inches in length over his right eye and there was a similar wound to the left side of his head. Blood was still flowing from them, which the doctor was able to stem before sending Gordon home.

The constable lodged locally at 178, Westfield Street, where he shared a room with shoemaker, Alexander Pratt. Gordon arrived there at just before three o'clock and seeing that his head was bandaged, his roommate asked if there was anything he could do for him. Gordon replied that he felt fine but asked to be woken up at eight, as he fully intended to report for duty. However, when Alex rose from his bed at seven, he realised immediately that Gordon had died. Dr McNichol arrived at Westfield Street, where he performed a post-mortem, which led him to conclude the deceased had died of heart failure caused by shock, which was brought on by the violence he had suffered the previous night.

During the night, Carney was charged with assault and the theft of hens, but he denied everything. Leahey had been apprehended at his home one hour after the break-in and he too denied any involvement.

Frank Riley. (The Illustrated Police News)

On his arrival at the police station, Gordon was still there and identified him as the one who had hit him with the iron bar, prompting Leahey to laugh out loudly. Riley was caught later that morning and insisted he knew nothing of the crime.

Nevertheless, when it became known during the day that Gordon was dead, Riley asked to make a new statement in which he said 'I was in the place and when the bobbies came, Gordon got hold of me. Whalley was keeping the other men away. They ran towards me and got me away. I don't know whether they hit Gordon or not. I had nothing in my hand and I used no violence' In making this statement, by which he clearly hoped to distance himself from the killing, Riley had, nevertheless, placed the three arrested men at the crime scene.

Gordon's burial took place at the St Helens Cemetery on 16 November and was attended by colleagues from the Liverpool, St Helens and surrounding forces, together with many townsfolk. A subscription fund raised £30, which was sent to his widowed mother in Scotland.

The trial of the three accused opened at the Liverpool Assizes on Friday March 16 and they were charged with murder and poultry theft. They were represented by Dr Andrew Commins MP, who at the close of the prosecution case addressed the jury. He submitted that the crown had failed to demonstrate who had struck the fatal blow or been able to show whether or not the deceased had exceeded his authority and used greater force than was necessary, in which case the accused would have been justified in offering resistance. He continued by suggesting that there was no definitive evidence that death was due to the injuries inflicted on the night in question and it should therefore be presumed that death was due to natural causes, namely heart failure. However, if the jury believed he had died due to the injuries he received that night, their barrister argued it was dark and in the confusion, Constable Whalley might have struck him accidentally. He concluded by stating that in his view it was impossible to convict any of his clients of murder.

In his summing up, it was obvious that the judge rejected the defence case. He described the behaviour of the officers as heroic and observed that despite a great deal of provocation, Gordon had not withdrawn his staff. Both had received injuries without having inflicted any of consequence on their attackers.

The jury retired for ninety minutes and returned a verdict of guilty on all matters but added a unanimous recommendation for mercy. As the judge placed the black cap on his head, several women in the courtroom began to call out the names of the accused and scream uncontrollably. Order was restored, but only with some difficulty and the convicted men were sentenced to death.

The men's solicitor, Henry Riley, initiated a campaign to seek a reprieve, for which it quickly became clear there was widespread support, as unsolicited letters signed by individuals and from organisations bearing many signatures began to arrive at his office. A number of reasons for this support was offered; the killing was not premeditated as

John Leahey. (The Illustrated Police News)

John Carney. (The Illustrated Police News)

the men carried no lethal weapons with them; they should have been given the benefit of the doubt regarding the possibility that Gordon may well have been struck accidentally in the dark and confined space by Whalley; it was possible that death had been due to heart failure for reasons other than the violent struggle in which the constable was involved; and it was felt by many that a further mitigating factor was that at the time, striking miners were suffering greatly as they had no wages coming in and were close to starvation.

One of the letters received by the solicitor was sent by a member of the jury who convicted the men, which read:

> 'I never believed they were responsible for the murder of Gordon and only agreed with the verdict on the condition that there was attached to it a recommendation to mercy, sufficiently strong to move the authorities' clemency. I paid much attention to the evidence given by the only living witness, that was the constable, and I was convinced that there was a doubt as to whether the prisoners were Gordon's murderers. The doctor who saw Gordon after the assault only confirmed me in the opinion, as the injuries were treated by him as trivial ones. I was also more confirmed, if possible, by the entry in the police charge book, in which the charge booked was entered as a common assault upon the police. I verily believe if the jury could have forgotten for the time being, the summing up of his lordship and his charge to the jury and have rested on the evidence they heard, they would never have arrived at the verdict they did. I certainly trust you will be successful in your efforts for a reprieve and shall be glad to supply you with any information in my power. I shall be very pleased to sign a petition.'

Support for the condemned men increased greatly when it became known that Leahey's mother had been denied entry into Walton Gaol on two occasions, despite having visiting orders, due to administrative errors. This had left her without sufficient funds to visit him before his approaching execution date.

Thirteen thousand signatures were gathered in support of reprieves and on the evening of 27 March, Mr Riley received the following telegraph:

> 'From the Under Secretary, Home Office, Whitehall. To Riley Solicitors, Claughton Chambers, St Helens. The Secretary of State has advised Her Majesty to respite the capital sentences passed on John Carney, John Leahey and Frank Riley, with a view to commutation.'

There was a great deal of rejoicing in the town that night and Fred Lucas, proprietor of the People's Palace Theatre, interrupted the show to advise the audience of the news, which was greeted with wild cheering. A few days later, it was announced that the three men would undergo fifteen years penal servitude.

Constable James Gordon has not been forgotten. One hundred and twenty years after his murder, his grave was by now unmarked, but with funds provided by The Police Roll of Honour Trust, a new headstone was commissioned. On 13 November 2013, this was unveiled in front of a large gathering of police officers and others, by Geraldine Winner, widow of film maker Michael Winner, who had established The Police Memorial Trust in 1984.

25

Detective Sergeant Robert Kidd
London & North Western Railway Police
1895

37-year-old Detective Sergeant Robert Kidd joined the police force of the London & North Western Railway Co. in 1885 as a constable and became a detective two years later, after which he served at Warrington and Edge Hill. Following his promotion to sergeant in 1889, he was transferred to Liverpool Road Station in Manchester. He was married with seven children and lived in Salford. On Sunday 29 September 1895, he boarded the seven o'clock train from Manchester and one

Detective Sergeant Robert Kidd. (The author)

hour later arrived at Wigan, where he was to offer assistance to local officer Detective Constable William Osborne.

For the previous two months there had been a great deal of pilfering from goods wagons in the sidings situated a few hundred yards from station. These offences usually took place at the weekend when no staff worked in the sidings and the two officers were to keep watch and if possible arrest those responsible. Within a few minutes of the sergeant's arrival, the two officers set off on foot for the sidings.

Osborne would later recall that as they approached the wagons, he saw a man and said, 'Hello there, what do you want?' There was a group of several men behind him and the man shouted towards them, 'Hey up lads, have you got them?' and then attempted to run away. Osborne gave chase and caught up with him which led to a violent struggle. Osborne was injured and lost consciousness momentarily, but saw that Kidd was in pursuit of the other men. As he was coming round, Osborne saw the men in the distance making their escape and Kidd on his hands and knees, clearly in distress. He approached him and Kidd muttered, 'Is that you Osborne? Get me a drink of water.' The constable attempted to carry his stricken colleague but was too weak to do so. He laid him down and crawled to No. 2 signal box, where he alerted Seth Rigby, who telephoned for assistance and an ambulance. Unfortunately, by the time it arrived, Kidd was dead.

His body was taken to the station, where it was placed in a waiting room. It was only now that it was realised he had been stabbed a number of times, thus becoming the first member of L&NWR staff to be murdered on duty, since its foundation in 1846. The badly injured constable was taken to the infirmary, where he would remain for five days and recover fully from his injuries over the next month.

When a search of the immediate area was made, two large pools of blood indicated how severe the struggle was that Kidd had with his killer. Also, two caps, saturated with blood, were found, which were presumed to have been worn by two members of the gang.

On just one of the wagons, the cords used to secure the cover had been cut and the contents disturbed. A bottle of chlorine of lozenges was lying on the ground, thought to have been dropped by the thieves as they fled. It was discovered that one bottle of sweets had been stolen. The murder weapon was not found and although a blood-stained knife was discovered sixty yards away on 3 November, this could not be said with any certainty to have been that weapon.

Within yards of the sidings was a terrace of workers' cottages and it was believed likely that many of the colliers who lived in them, supplemented their wages with the proceeds of thefts from the railway wagons. The police acted quickly and in the early hours of the Sunday morning, the cottages were surrounded and each of them was subjected to a thorough search. Several suspects were taken into custody, among them William Kearsley, who had a lengthy list of court appearances for railway thefts and he had also served a lengthy prison sentence for a serious assault on a gamekeeper. The suspects were taken to the infirmary, where they were brought to Osborne's bedside. Without hesitation, the constable identified Kearsley as one of the gang. After further questioning, the other men were released and only Kearsley held in custody. However, by now the police had gathered information that would lead to two further arrests.

A post-mortem revealed the sergeant bled to death; there were nine stab wounds to his head, face and neck; his jugular vein had been severed; there was a large wound to his right cheek; and his nose was almost slit in two. The tip of his left index finger had been sliced off as he attempted to defend himself and there were many cuts and bruises to his body.

The investigation, which was being conducted jointly by the Wigan police and detectives from the LNWR, received important information from collier Richard Pritchard, one of the men arrested originally and later released. He recalled meeting Kearsley and his brother-in-law Elijah Winstanley together with William Halliwell in the New Inn at six o'clock on the evening of the murder. The four men left the pub and Pritchard parted from the other three, close to the railway sidings and he continued on his way home. He could not say definitely if the others entered the sidings, but he had confirmed they were nearby at about the time of the murder.

Halliwell was arrested on the Tuesday morning and taken to the infirmary, where Osborne picked him out from a group of six men as the thief with whom he had fought. Winstanley was also arrested but told the officers, 'I know nothing about it.' He too was taken to the infirmary to stand before Osborne. The constable was only able to say he resembled one of the men but added that he had hit that man on the right hand with his truncheon, when he had approached with the intention of helping Halliwell and it was noted that Winstanley had a swollen and heavily bruised right thumb.

The police believed they now had the three men who bore most responsibility for Kidd's death and on the following Thursday they appeared before the town's magistrates, all charged with murdering Kidd and assaulting Osborne. They were placed in the dock and almost immediately Winstanley became extremely agitated and screamed, 'Kill me, kill me. Go on, it's murder! I did it, I did it! It's me! I didn't intend killing him.' Then, pointing towards Kearsley, his brother-in-law, he added, 'It's not our Bill.'

He calmed down eventually, but the drama continued in the packed courtroom, when the prosecution announced that the murder charge against Halliwell was to be withdrawn. It had been accepted that he was fighting with Osborne and this was at some distance from the stabbing when it took place and that he had not known any of his friends had a knife. He would be charged only with inflicting grievous bodily harm in the case of Osborne. It was then stated that he would be testifying against Winstanley and Kearsley at the forthcoming trial on behalf of the crown. Halliwell was then removed from the dock.

The prosecution outlined its case and noted that Kearsley was identified by Osborne and witnesses had seen him wearing one of the caps discovered at the murder scene, earlier in the evening. As far as Winstanley was concerned, another of the caps had been shown to belong to him and a pair of blood stained clogs were found when his house was searched. There were also the injuries to his right hand, which it was claimed had been inflicted by Osborne.

There was uproar once again when Halliwell returned to the witness box to give his account of events after Richard Pritchard left them and he and the two others reached the sidings. They climbed over a fence into the goods yard and approached the wagons not knowing what they contained but hoping there would be something they could use themselves or possibly sell. Kearsley told the witness to keep watch and within minutes, Osborne appeared and they began to struggle. Kidd ran past them in the direction of the other two defendants. After a few minutes, Halliwell made good his escape and went to the Fox Tavern, where he met Kearsley and Winstanley. He claimed Winstanley said the officer had grabbed him and pulled him to the ground and added, 'I do not think he will live, I stabbed him many times.'

Another prosecution witness was Kearsley's daughter Elizabeth, who recalled her father coming home late on that Sunday night. Her evidence incriminated her father in the planned theft and confirmed his presence in the sidings, but it did suggest he had not been involved in the stabbing. She heard her parents talking and her father saying, 'Our Elijah has been stabbing a bobby in the face and neck with a knife'. At the close of the hearing, Winstanley and Kearsley were committed to the next Liverpool Assizes charged with murder and Halliwell with assault.

Their trial was held on 29 November at which both Kearsley and Winstanley pleaded not guilty. Kearsley insisted he had fled the scene before the stabbing took place and the crown accepted he might not have actually stabbed the sergeant. However, it was believed that Kidd must have been held down for the fatal injuries to have been inflicted and only Kearsley could have done this, which would be confirmed by Halliwell. Winstanley admitted stabbing Kidd but argued that he was acting in self-defence as excessive violence was being used against him by the sergeant, who was in plain clothes, meaning he did not realise at the time that he was a police officer.

Halliwell's testimony could not be easily dismissed, despite the defence suggesting it was tainted as he was simply attempting to save himself. Nevertheless, he repeated the account he gave before the magistrates, but it was obvious that the emotional stress of acting as an informer against former friends in front of many neighbours, who were packed into the court, was taking its toll. Speaking in a hushed, barely audible voice, he was a miserable figure, whose face was now deathly pale.

At the conclusion of the evidence, the jury remained in the courtroom as they discussed the case for fifteen minutes, after which they found both defendants guilty of wilful murder. When the now convicted men were asked by the judge if they had anything to say,

Kearsley repeated his claim of innocence and Winstanley said, 'It was me as did it. Our Bill never touched him, he ran away. I did it and that's God's truth.' They were then sentenced to death and taken to Liverpool's Walton Gaol to await their executions.

The next day, Halliwell was brought into the dock supposedly to face his trial. However, the crown's barrister advised the judge that it had been decided not to proceed with the charges of assaulting Osborne. The judge agreed with this decision and he instructed the jury to acquit him on all matters. Halliwell was discharged and left the court a free man.

Petitions seeking reprieves for both of the condemned men were organised by their solicitor, James Wilson. As far as Kearsley was concerned it was noted that the only incriminating evidence against him was provided by Halliwell, an unreliable witness. Furthermore, Winstanley had always said his brother-in-law was not in any way responsible for the detective's death and following the trial he had made a full written confession, acknowledging his own guilt, describing Halliwell as a liar and exonerating Kearsley.

As for Winstanley, the petition focused on the absence of premeditation and malice aforethought. Also, apart from two minor previous offences he was a man of good character, industrious and sober and known to be a good husband and father.

Both petitions were well supported and the solicitor received the following two letters, supporting his campaign, in respect of Kearsley:

'Dear Sir, As one of the jurors in the sad and unfortunate case, I had with other jurors some doubt in my mind as to the probability of William Kearsley having actually assisted Winstanley in the tragic affair and I believe had it not been for the evidence given by the prisoner Halliwell, I would have given Kearsley the benefit of the doubt. On hearing, after our verdict had been given, the assertion of Winstanley, it certainly made me think that it was to be relied upon, but of course our verdict has been given. The Home Secretary will carefully review the whole case. With this doubt in my mind I should have no hesitation in signing the petition on behalf of Kearsley.'

The second jury member wrote the following:

> 'Dear Sir, I was unfortunate enough to be one of the jurors at the recent Liverpool Assizes who found Winstanley and Kearsley guilty of the murder of Detective Kidd at Wigan and was the last to fall in with the decision of the others s to Kearsley's guilt, being influenced thereto by evidence given by Halliwell. Winstanley's after declaration of Kearsley's innocence brought back my doubt and I also shall be glad to sign the petition which you are about to present to the Home Secretary.'

Mr Wilson was only partially successful as Kearsley was reprieved and his sentence commuted to life imprisonment. Winstanley however, was not so fortunate and it was decided that his execution should proceed as planned on 17 December. The authorities feared, that given his fragile state of mind Winstanley would perhaps pose many problems at his hanging which was to be carried out by James Billington. However, these fears proved to be misplaced and he died penitent and showed great courage.

Walton Gaol. (The author)

When notified of his reprieve, Kearsley wrote from Walton Gaol to his wife:

> 'Dear Wife, you will have seen the papers that I have been reprieved and that the death sentence will not be carried out. I need hardly say to you that it is a great blessing and for which I am most thankful as I know you are also. I hardly know what to say to you, but trust that we may be spared to meet again. I will do my best in order that I may gain every advantage my sentence will allow. I hope you will do as well as you can and that God will bless you and the children and spare us to meet again. I will be allowed a visit and should like you to come if you can and if not some of the family must come. You will not require to go to the police station this time. Go straight to the prison. I will finish this letter with best love to you, the children and all friends. I will tell you what I want most when you come to see me. Your affectionate husband, WM, KEARSLEY.'

Kearsley proved to be a model prisoner and he continued to receive the support of his solicitor Mr Wilson who was in continuous contact with the Home Office and in a letter to his wife dated, 17 November 1902, sent from Dartmoor Prison, he wrote:

> 'Dear Wife, I am in good health and I hope you and the children are so too. I am glad to tell you that I shall be home in the middle of February. Will you please let all my friends know this, especially Uncle James. I will write again about Christmas time. Yours affectionately, WILLIAM KEARSLEY'

After serving seven years and three months, the now 48-year-old Kearsley arrived in Wigan on the night of Saturday 7 February 1903. He was met by a large number of family, friends and well-wishers, but having promised four years earlier never to touch a drop of alcohol again, he declined all offers of a celebratory drink. On the Monday morning, accompanied by his wife, he visited the office of his solicitor, Mr Wilson, to thank him for the support he had given him over the years.

26

Constable Ernest Thompson
Metropolitan Police
1900

32-year-old Constable Ernest Thompson had served with the Metropolitan Police since 1890 and was based at Leman Street Police Station. He had first come to the notice of the public in February 1891, when in the early hours of the thirteenth, he had discovered the body of Frances Coles in Swallow Gardens. Her throat had been cut from ear to ear and at the time, the police believed she was possibly a victim of Jack the Ripper. Almost a decade later, shortly after midnight Saturday 1 December 1900, he was on his beat, part of which included the district around Church Lane, Union Street and Commercial Road in

Constable Ernest Thompson. (The author)

Whitechapel. This was an area in which there were a number of brothels, acts of violence were commonplace and so too were many other crimes.

At twenty minutes to one, Constable Thompson met William Ward on Commercial Road. Ward was a labourer who had been a warder at Pentonville Prison previously and the two men knew each other well. They had been talking for ten minutes, when a group of seven men and two women approached. They were in a boisterous mood and were singing and chatting loudly. The constable ordered them to be quiet or he would call for assistance and arrest them all for causing a disturbance.

They quietened down and walked away except for one of the men. This was 41-year-old Barnet Abrahams, a cigar maker, who lived in Mile End. Angry and using the foulest of language, he demanded to know what he had done wrong and the group of friends who had just left returned, apparently to offer him their support and they too were now in a menacing mood. Eventually, the constable was able to persuade them to walk away. William Ward also left and Thompson continued on his beat.

William Butcher had a stall in the neighbourhood, selling coffee and hot food, which was open between midnight and seven in the morning. At one o'clock, Abrahams and the two women came and he ordered coffee, eggs, bread and butter for the women, which he paid for, but nothing for himself. Once more, they began singing loudly, which attracted the attention of Thompson. He again ordered them to be quiet and to go home, which the women did immediately, but Abrahams demanded, 'What have I done?' He continued to argue for a few minutes more, before walking away towards Union Street, followed by the constable.

William Butcher watched as the pair walked a short distance along the street, the constable following a few paces behind Abrahams, who suddenly stopped and turned to confront him. They drew closer and began to struggle, before falling to the ground. Coincidentally, seven constables were escorting five prisoners to Arbour Square Police Station and they too had seen the confrontation. Several of them rushed to the spot, among them Constables Pimms, Beckett and Atkinson, to offer what assistance they could. They arrived to see their colleague kneeling on Abrahams, but by now blood was pouring from a neck wound and he told them, 'I am done, he has stabbed me. Hold him.'

More officers arrived, with truncheons drawn and Abrahams was struck a number of blows to his face, head and upper body before his pocket-knife, the blade of which was open and blood-stained was taken from him. He was taken under escort to Leman Street and Constable Thompson was taken by cab to the London Hospital, but he was dead on arrival. A post mortem was carried out by Francis

Hillyard, a surgeon at the hospital, who found a knife wound to the left side of the neck, which had severed the carotid artery and jugular vein. This had led to a considerable loss of blood, which was the cause of death. He confirmed that in his opinion the knife found at the scene was probably the weapon responsible for the fatal injuries.

On his arrival at the station it was seen that Abrahams bore the marks of a severe beating and as he was being taken to a cell, he complained, 'They nearly murdered me with them truncheons and it is a wonder I am alive.' The officers who had brought him there, insisted he had put up a violent struggle as they were attempting to arrest him and it had been necessary to use a great deal of force. Later that morning at seven o'clock, the prisoner was brought before Detective Inspector Thomas Davill, who advised him of the constable's death and charged him with his murder. The accused man remained calm and told the inspector, 'It is possible, but I don't remember anything about it. I had no cause to do any injury to anybody.' Later he said, 'I regret it but it can't be helped.'

The inquest into the officer's death opened at the London Hospital on Monday 3 December, by which time the Cigar Makers Association, of which the accused was a member, had hired the well-known and much respected solicitor, Charles Deakin to represent him at this stage and to arrange for counsel at his forthcoming trial. Abrahams was brought to the hospital entrance in a cab from Leman Street and on his arrival, he was met by a large and hostile crowd, who hissed and booed him loudly.

The two women who were with Abrahams in the minutes leading up to the stabbing were never identified or traced. However, the coroner's jury heard evidence from William Butcher, Francis Hillyard and the police officers who had gone to the dead man's aid. William Ward was called to testify, but Mr Deakin had learnt that he had met with a journalist from one of the capital's evening newspapers and had been paid for doing so. This was not denied, but Ward insisted he had not been encouraged to embellish his account in order to make the story more interesting. It also emerged under further questioning that the witness had been dismissed from the prison service because of unpunctuality. By the time he stepped out of the witness box, many in the court were laughing loudly and the crown would not call on him to testify at any future hearing, including the trial, given the unreliability of his account.

The coroner's jury found that the deceased had been wilfully murdered by Abrahams and a similar conclusion was reached the following week, when he appeared before the magistrates at the Thames Police Court. He was therefore committed to stand trial at the Old Bailey.

The dead officer was interred at Bow Cemetery and his coffin bore a plaque inscribed 'Ernest Thompson departed this life December 1 1900, aged 32 years'. The mourners were led by his widow and their four children, all aged under five and a large number of Metropolitan Police officers were present. The route of the cortège, which left his house in Stepney, was lined with hundreds of residents, eager to show their respects and shopkeepers closed their premises as the procession passed by.

His widow was entitled to a small pension and a fund, supported by the MPs for Stepney and Whitechapel together with several local churchmen, was opened. Within a few days, it was announced that £167 had already been raised from individuals and organisations and donations continued to be received.

The funeral of the dead officer. (The Illustrated Police News)

On 2 February, what would prove to be the last trial of an individual accused of murdering a police officer in the Victorian age, opened at the Old Bailey and Abrahams entered a not guilty plea, claiming the fatal wound had been caused accidentally. His barrister insisted that some of the injuries the accused suffered on that night were inflicted by the deceased, who as the two men struggled, had punched, kicked and struck him with his truncheon. This had caused his client to fall to the ground and the constable had fallen on top of him and on to the knife, which was open, in Abrahams' pocket. This argument was rejected by the crown and Constable David Tittle was called to testify. He swore that his colleague's truncheon was still in his pocket on arrival at the London Hospital, meaning he could not have used it to hit the accused.

William Ellis, a cab washer, who visited William Butcher's stall for a cup of coffee on the night of the stabbing, also appeared for the defence. He testified that he believed the constable acted with a great deal of aggression towards the defendant just before they fell to the ground and his evidence may have influenced the jury, who found Abrahams not guilty of murder but convicted him of manslaughter, which suggests they rejected much of his account but accepted he had been provoked to some extent. He was sentenced to twenty years penal servitude.

Charles Deakin, the 43-year-old solicitor, who had acted for Abrahams following his arrest, did not assist the defence barrister at the trial. He had been arrested on serious criminal charges and appeared at the Old Bailey a few weeks later on 13 May. An investigation into his affairs revealed that he had fraudulently converted the £53 15s paid to him by the Cigar Makers Association towards the defence of Abrahams, to his own use. The subsequent police investigation into his affairs had uncovered other examples of malpractice. In one instance, it was discovered he had been handed £200 by Captain W Hay of the Union Castle Line to invest on his behalf, but the solicitor had used the money for his own purposes. Deakin pleaded guilty and was sentenced to five years penal servitude.

In the summer of 1911, Abrahams died following what was described as an apoplectic seizure whilst working in the yard of Parkhurst Prison.

Sources and Bibliography

Bent, Superintendent James, *Criminal Life; Reminiscences of Forty-Two Years as a Police Officer,* J Heywood, 1891 Berry, James, *My Experiences as an Executioner,* P Lund, 1892

The Ashton Weekly Reporter
The Barnsley Chronicle
Bristol Times and Mirror
The Burnley Advertiser
Bury Times
Chelmsford Chronicle
The Daily Gazette for Middlesbrough
The Daily News
The Durham Chronicle
East London Observer
The Essex Herald
The Fife Free Press
Fifeshire Advertiser
The Freeman's Journal
The Glasgow Herald
The Illustrated Police News
The Lancaster Gazette
Liverpool Mercury
The Manchester Courier and Lancashire General Advertiser
The Manchester Weekly Times
The Morning Post
The Pall Mall Gazette
Reading Mercury
Shipping and Mercantile Gazette
South Wales Daily News

The Standard (London)
The Warminster and Westbury Journal
Western Mail
The Wigan Observer
The Worcestershire Chronicle
The Yorkshire Post

I also used the online resources of the following
The British Newspaper Archive
The National Archives
Old Bailey Proceedings

Index

INDEX